Eu

'… I love Jacky's Books!' – **Melissa Porter, TV presenter**

'Jacky's writing has inspired me in so many ways. She is and always will be an Angel in my eyes.' – **TV's *Psychic Medium*, Barrie John**

'… Jacky Newcomb's books have made her a well-respected name in the study of angels and afterlife communication. Jacky's work is essential reading for anyone interested in learning more about this fascinating subject …' – **Uri Geller**

'My mind has always been open to life beyond this life … if yours isn't, read Jacky Newcomb's books … and if it is … just enjoy!' – **Suzi Quatro, musician, singer/songwriter, actor, author, TV and radio presenter**

'… Whenever I meet people in the course of my work [who are] interested in angels, I point them in Jacky's direction – she is the fountain of all "angel" knowledge. I know her books have helped so many.' – **Tony Stockwell, TV's *Psychic Medium* and best-selling author**

'If you want to know anything about angels, then Jacky Newcomb's books are a great place to start; they always make me smile with such inspiring and uplifting true-life tales of angelic encounters. Jacky has been researching this subject for many years so knows her stuff; she is truly passionate about angels!' – **Katy Evans, editor *Soul & Spirit* magazine**

'Jacky writes inspirational books and articles about angels, all from the heart, spiritual and enlightening …' – ***Woman's Weekly***

'… Jacky Newcomb has established a reputation as one of the country's leading paranormal experiences experts …' – ***Staffordshire Life* magazine**

'No matter what your beliefs are, you can't help but feel hope that there is something beyond the certainty of death. Personally, I felt deeply touched by a number of the stories in Jacky's book and I felt reassured and calmed by her approach in relaying these messages from beyond! The book itself, like the lady, is approachable and friendly.' – **Marion Davies, Managing Director *SimplyHealth247* magazine**

'First of all, cancel out all notions of veils, crystal balls, and associated ghostly, pantomime-style antics. Contrary to popular misconceptions, Jacky Newcomb is a non-cloak-wearing, wingless, very pleasant lady who, by her own admission, leads what she considers a very "ordinary" life …' – ***Exclusive* magazine**

Healed by an Angel

Jacky Newcomb

HAY HOUSE

Australia • Canada • Hong Kong • India
South Africa • United Kingdom • United States

First published and distributed in the United Kingdom by:
Hay House UK Ltd, 292B Kensal Rd, London W10 5BE. Tel.: (44) 20 8962 1230;
Fax: (44) 20 8962 1239. www.hayhouse.co.uk

Published and distributed in the United States of America by:
Hay House, Inc., PO Box 5100, Carlsbad, CA 92018-5100. Tel.: (1) 760 431 7695 or
(800) 654 5126; Fax: (1) 760 431 6948 or (800) 650 5115. www.hayhouse.com

Published and distributed in Australia by:
Hay House Australia Ltd, 18/36 Ralph St, Alexandria NSW 2015.
Tel.: (61) 2 9669 4299; Fax: (61) 2 9669 4144. www.hayhouse.com.au

Published and distributed in the Republic of South Africa by:
Hay House SA (Pty), Ltd, PO Box 990, Witkoppen 2068. Tel./Fax: (27) 11 467 8904.
www.hayhouse.co.za

Published and distributed in India by:
Hay House Publishers India, Muskaan Complex, Plot No.3, B-2, Vasant Kunj,
New Delhi – 110 070. Tel.: (91) 11 4176 1620; Fax: (91) 11 4176 1630.
www.hayhouse.co.in

Distributed in Canada by:
Raincoast, 9050 Shaughnessy St, Vancouver, BC V6P 6E5. Tel.: (1) 604 323 7100;
Fax: (1) 604 323 2600

A catalogue record for this book is available from the British Library.

ISBN 978-1-84850-296-3

Printed in the UK by CPI Bookmarque, Croydon, CR0 4TD.

Contents

Letter to My Readers

Dear Readers

This special collection of stories is my twelfth published book and I have enjoyed every minute of writing and researching it for you. Over the years I have only grown more and more fascinated with everything related to the paranormal, especially angels and the afterlife ... of course!

Recently my husband and I moved to Cornwall in England. We had been drawn here for many years and finally the timing was right. It was a serious upheaval to transport our many belongings (including two cats) to our new location, but Cornwall is such a magical place that it had to be done. I felt drawn here as if to a magnet, and I realize it's no good suggesting to my readers that they should follow their instincts if I don't do the same, now is it?

The only sad part was that we left most of our family (including our two daughters and later a new granddaughter) in the Midlands (several hours' drive away) ... I am hoping the experience helps them to grow spiritually and, as you would imagine, we've prepared a luxuriously appointed spare bedroom ... to encourage lengthy visits! We also spend many hours on the telephone ... and computer – webcams are brilliant!

In our new home I am extremely spoiled. The property is off a quiet lane surrounded by tall hedges and mature trees. A near neighbour keeps exotic birds and, although I'm not sure what birds he keeps, I can hear them calling each morning and evening. The sound is quite exquisite and I often imagine I live in the middle of a tropical jungle!

Our home is high up on a hill and our bedroom window offers the most amazing view. It's the best place to watch the sun setting and the colours can be quite breathtaking. I love to watch as the sparrows swarm over the house each evening and sing in the treetops in the garden.

We live 20 minutes from the sea and within a short drive there's the opportunity to walk along many beaches – such a blessing. We love to collect driftwood from the seashore to bring home for log fires! As the weather picks up I am hoping we can make more use of the local facilities. In the meantime a local spa offers the use of a wonderful pool and, best of all ... a hot tub! Much inspiration comes to me as I sit and relax there ... I highly recommend it.

If I choose to stay at home, we have a pretty garden. As I look out of my window the lawn is filled with thousands of snowdrops ... a gift from the previous occupant! Pots of herbs surround the front door and I can't wait to plant up scented flowers ... the smell of which should then greet anyone who visits as they arrive and leave. Naturally garden statues (angels, of course) also sit by the door to greet guests ... just in case they weren't sure if they were at the right house! My husband John has carved a piece of slate with the words 'Angel Haven' – it is indeed! My favourite statue is of a little angel who sits cross-legged reading a book. What better than a book-angel for an author?

My writing room is a gift. It's larger than the living room of our old house; I purchased a large desk especially which surrounds me on two sides. I have many shelves for books ... particularly for research purposes, you understand! Everything that can be is decorated with images of angels, including my clock, drink coasters, candles, notebooks and dishes for angel cards. I have display cabinets filled with beautiful crystals, incense and angel statues. I have collections of angel coins, blessing stones and sprays of angel essences and oils (mainly gifts from fans and friends) to energize my room. On the top of one cabinet I have an ever-changing arrangement of favourite things: a little angel altar. This year fans have sent me angel books, crystals, angel figurines, jewellery and two knitted angels ... thank you all! I am honoured to receive your gifts.

This room also holds a beautiful pine cabinet with a glass front and it's full of, yes, you guessed it: more angels. This time they are smaller versions of crystal angels (made of semi-precious stones) and tiny gifts (including teeny-tiny angel books) and aromatherapy oils.

Finally pride of place is given to framed photographs of me and the dear friends whom I've met along my journey. I also have photographs of me with some special fans ... wonderful new friends who come to my talks and workshops around the country (bless you all).

My husband bought me a lovely meditation chair as a gift. It has a matching stool and vibrates to encourage relaxation ... my life is complete! I do have to fight the cat for this chair, though ... my big ginger tom, Tigger, is under the illusion that it belongs to him. My little black cat usually sits on the top tier of my in-tray ... both cats are never far away.

So here I sit at my massive desk, researching and writing my books for you, dear reader, for without you there would be no books at all. I have welcomed, and continue to welcome, your own personal paranormal and mystical experiences. Thank you for sharing them with me. I would also like to take this opportunity to thank you for your continued support and welcome feedback to my books. I know that some of you have read everything I have written, and that is very humbling!

Now we begin another journey. This time we concentrate a little more on the stories of healing and hospitals ... experiences from healers, carers and nurses. Angels come in many guises, but this latest collection of stories is just a little bit magical! As always I have shared angel stories of all sorts ... just to bring a little enchantment into your life. Thank you for joining me.

Angel Blessings

Jacky x

Welcome to My Spooky Life

Tell me not, in mournful numbers,
Life is but an empty dream!
For the soul is dead that slumbers,
and things are not what they seem.
– Henry Wadsworth Longfellow

'Mum, I've got something to tell you ...' my eldest daughter, 21-year-old Charlotte said cautiously.

'Go ahead!' I replied, curious. Then just as suddenly she seemed to change her mind.

'I can't ... maybe Granddad will tell you?' She seemed unsure.

There's nothing wrong with Charlotte's granddad sharing her news, except for one thing ... Granddad, my father, is dead! Yet in our house, the dead communicate almost as much as the living. Being dead doesn't stop our relatives from calling in to chat on a regular basis! We think of our deceased relatives as our guardian angels, watching over us and certainly keeping an eye on our lives down here on Earth.

Charlotte jumped up and rushed into the other room where we kept an angel board … a type of Ouija Board™/spirit board, our chosen method of communication. It sounds scary but spirit boards are a wonderful form of communicating with the afterlife. All those stories you read about negative experiences from using spirit-type boards … well, I've never encountered anything like that in my life and I have been using them (somewhat controversially) for years. People are frightened of them because basically they work. They really are a communication tool for reaching out to the other side of life.

I always follow a ritual of love and protection followed by a prayer before I start using them … better safe than sorry! Placing the board on the table, Charlotte and I put our fingers onto the glass, waiting for it to begin moving across the board, which is covered in letters and numbers. The way these boards work is that the glass (or pointer/planchette) moves over the letters and numbers, spelling out messages. This time was no exception and the glass began to stir into life, gliding over the letters. I glanced up at Charlotte to see if she was going to talk to me, but she was looking down firmly.

'Hi Granddad, are you there?'

'Yes'

'Will you tell Mum, please?'

I was full of curiosity. What on Earth was wrong? What could my adult daughter have to tell me that was so terrible that she couldn't tell me herself? I'll admit by this stage I was really concerned. There was nothing for it but to look down and follow the movements of the glass. As it shifted over the letters I began to write them down.

Slowly the pointer started to spell: *P*. I added it to the notebook beside me. *R E* I wrote these letters down as well. *G* ... Then it became glaringly obvious ...

'You're pregnant?' I asked in surprise. I'm not sure now why I was surprised. She was 21 with her own home and a partner of four years' standing! 'You're pregnant?' I asked again, trying to hide the excitement in my voice.

'I thought you'd be cross ...'

'Cross?' I looked at my daughter, so suddenly young, and rushed over to hug her close. 'I'm delighted!' I rushed on – then it hit me: I'd be a grandma at 48! 'Wow!'

Over the years we've often used a spirit board (well, an Angel Board, which is slightly different in that it's illustrated with angels and the intent is to communicate with only the highest realms of heaven) to reach out to many of our loved ones on the other side. Readers of my other books will have heard all about our communication with Eric (my dad's brother) and more recently Dad, who is a more recent passing, as well as a whole list of deceased family and friends.

My own deceased loved ones have appeared during séance-type sessions like the mini one Charlotte and I enacted here, and they have also materialized in dream-visitations ... real visits from their spirits, but when I was asleep. If you've never had an experience like this before, let me tell you that these real visits from deceased loved ones are like no other dream you've had before ... let me explain.

A deceased loved one (a family member, friend, colleague, etc.) will walk into a dream. Yes, honestly, one minute you're dreaming a normal dream and then just as suddenly the dream passes on by. You know the way sections of a film are joined together to make a movie? Well, it's a little like this. One minute you're dreaming and then the next a new scene is blended into view, or merged in or (as I have experienced myself), the old view is pushed to one side and the new 'visitation' is slid into the frame! Weird. The result is a communication from spirits of the deceased. They walk in to chat to us.

THE DREAM-VISITATION
Let me explain further. The souls of our deceased relatives have the ability to 'visit' us when we are asleep. For various technical reasons (which we don't really understand), they come to us usually during our dream-sleep phase (REM sleep). The spirit of the deceased literally walks (flies or hovers) into a dream for a chat ... yes, even though they are dead!

It's common to have normal dreams about a loved one who has passed over, but these dream-visitations are different in many ways. If you've had a dream-visit from a deceased loved one you'll probably realize it by running through this list:

- **You feel lucid and aware. The experience is clear and unlike the muddled experience of a 'normal' dream.**
- **You remember the experience clearly when you wake up, although you might not recall everything you discussed (some conversations are about the deceased sharing information about what is coming up in your life ... reassuring you. It's information for your unconscious only). However, you will recall the actual experience for many years to come.**

- When you first see the loved one in this visit, you may be confused to see them 'alive'. You might even say to them something like, 'Why are you here? Aren't you dead?'
- They may symbolically show you that they are still alive (appearing in a hospital bed and having a doctor or nurse saying 'Look, they are alive after all', or sitting inside a coffin with the lid up and chatting to you!).
- They may walk through a type of fog (or white light) to get to you, or walk through a door or gate (or similar symbol, to show the passage from one space to another). You may see them cross over a bridge, for example.
- Other signs include those that show the difference between one vibrational 'level' and another (the difference between where they are in heaven and where we are on Earth): common are things like steps and stairs or even a lift, escalator or multi-storey car park! They are on a higher level and move down to greet you, you climb up/rise up or fly up, and you meet them somewhere in the middle.
- It's common for your loved one to appear younger than when they died (if they were older than 30 they will appear to be around that age) or if they were younger than 30 this will reflect the years since they passed, to indicate that they've 'grown up' in the spirit realm.
- Although your loved one can appear in any way they want to, they usually show themselves to you at their best: favourite hairstyle, wearing their favourite earthly outfit or the sort of thing they would have loved to have owned.
- Our loved ones appear without any signs of the illness or accident which may have caused their passing.

- They no longer need wigs, false teeth, walking sticks or glasses.
- They may be accompanied by a spirit guide or guardian angel.
- They might bring through other relatives or loved ones (sometimes to show they are looking after younger deceased children or babies).
- Pets may be collected and brought with them on the visit (my own father once appeared with every family dog we had ever owned!).

WHY DO THEY COME?

Loved ones visit for many reasons, but here are just a few of the more common ones:

- To reassure you that they are safe and well in their new dimension (in heaven).
- To let you know they didn't get lost and have met up with other deceased loved ones on the other side (we fear that they are alone … they're not).
- To tell you they loved you (especially if they didn't do this in life or because you weren't around to make that final goodbye).
- To reassure you that other loved ones on the other side are safe and well (especially if you have lost children; they want to reassure you that the child is being taken care of in the heavenly realms).
- To let you know they are proud of you and aware of your earthly achievements (as in, 'I wish Dad knew that I finally

passed my driving test. He would have been so proud of me.' He knows and he is!).

- So that you know they will still be at the wedding, christening, award ceremony, etc. In fact they occasionally appear in the photographs taken at these special occasions. Look out for fog-like mist, orbs (circles of light) or even actual faces which you weren't expecting, appearing on your printed photographs! I've even seen photographs with angel-type outlines and streaks of light which almost spell out letters or numbers!

- To reassure you that everything will be OK (during your own earthly crisis). Your loved one will like to pop back to tell you that things are not as bad as they seem, or let you know that the outcome of your current situation will be favourable.

- To warn you of danger (acting as a guardian angel); this is most likely to be a warning dream or actual words shouted in your ear ('stop', 'slow down', 'wake up', etc.).

- To help with healing (sitting with you when you are in hospital or at the scene of an accident).

I have stories which reflect this amazing phenomenon sprinkled throughout this book. Also, for the purposes of this book I encompass angels of all sorts: Angels in the traditional sense (Archangels from the Bible, for example), spirit guardians (maybe from other dimensions or realms) and deceased loved ones. How could I leave out angels of any sort? As you read about the experiences, see if there are stories that remind you of experiences of your own ... I bet you'll be reminded of something you'd hidden away at the back of your mind!

DEFINITION OF AN ANGEL

In the Bible (including the Hebrew Bible) and the Quran, an angel is a messenger of God. The word 'angel' comes from the Old English word *engel* and the Old French word *angele* (and the Latin *angelus* ... coming from the ancient Greek word *angelos*). Other words include the biblical *Elohim* ('God's messenger') and *Yahweh* ('messenger of the Lord'). Over time the word has come to mean a good spirit who watches over humankind ... these days we use the word 'angel' to include good human spirits (living or deceased), as in 'Oh, you're an angel!'

So really, an angel can be someone alive who acts in an angelic way, but mostly there is a little mysticism about the whole thing and it's more likely that the angel, your angel, is someone who appears only in dreams or whispers words to you when you are in danger or in great need. Together we'll explore many stories of all different types!

BACK TO DAD'S MESSAGE

Weeks passed after Charlotte and I had used the Angel Board and my daughter wanted to know the sex of the baby. It was too early for a scan but we wondered if Granddad might be able to help? Once again the glass moved over the letters, this time spelling out, IT'S A GIRL. A couple of months later, the official scan confirmed this.

MORE ABOUT MY WORK

My work covers all sorts of weird and wonderful things. I've spent much of my life researching aspects of the paranormal. As well as angels I also cover the afterlife, afterlife communication, life between lives, life after life, near-death experiences, out-of-body experiences, psychic children and life on other worlds ... aliens! There is much confusion between alien visits and angel visits (there's a book in there somewhere!).

You never know when a specific trail will lead to some new and fascinating discovery about the paranormal or the unknown. It's all linked anyway. I'm often running down one spiritual road and bumping into phenomena from another road entirely! A person who has a near-death experience might go on to see a deceased relative. Yet another who has an out-of-body experience during an accident or illness might see their guardian angel. Someone who 'dreams' they encounter a being from another world might be shown a previous life they've had. Where does one subject end and the next begin? To make sure I miss nothing, I read and research it all – I want my readers to know about everything that I do and, rest assured, if it's worth knowing I'll write about it for you!

My fascination lies with the real-life paranormal experience. Science doesn't interest me much, if I'm honest. Science is useful but it changes our life view all the time. It's easy as a human being to have a set of beliefs and then years later science discovers we were all wrong after all. Belief is only based on what we currently know to be true, so keeping an open mind is just good common sense, right? Let's keep exploring together!

You, my readers, are amazing. So many of you write and share your own mystical encounters and I learn new things from you all the time. From your letters I know that many of you would give up your jobs and learn about this phenomenon full time if you could. But I know you can't, so I'm happy to do this for you ... I'll just write about the good bits, OK?

By reading thousands and thousands of real-life experiences I began to notice patterns emerging from the data and, while you can say that it's all subjective, there are stories where even the spirits themselves will give the answer to a question which then finds its way to my postbag, and ultimately into a book. Mostly the stories come to me spontaneously through my website. Fans share their own spirit encounters voluntarily (and if this is you, then I want to thank you for that).

I also pick up occasional stories on social network sites such as Facebook and Twitter (used with permission). If you're not a member of these sites then please join me. I have a Facebook 'like page' (link on my website). It's also a good way to contact me directly.

Letters (and wonderful gifts from fans) also arrive in the post via my publishers. You can imagine the beautiful angels, crystals and spiritual products which find their way to me. I keep everything and display it in my home office (which doubles up as my meditation space). Letters and gifts also come to me via the magazines I write for. Again please may I just take a moment here and say thank you? I treasure every gift and they all add to the energy in my writing room.

I also read for hours every day; my favourite subjects are real-life paranormal experiences, as mentioned. The books I read come from all over the world (some of them are obscure self-published titles which are hard to find) ... it all helps to build up the picture. Please join me or feel free to share your own stories. You can also visit my website (see the back of this book for more details).

I began to get a feel for these experiences and, along with those I've had myself (of which there are plenty) and those shared with me by my own family, I became an accidental expert. They say, don't they, that the best career is when you are doing something you would be doing for free anyway? For me, this is it! Even on holiday, my beach-time reading is about paranormal phenomena!

So, to spread the word, I am involved with all sorts of things: theatre events, filmed shows, workshops, book signings, talks, etc. If and where possible I want to be involved with creating new products, and the plan for this year is more TV. Here is what I have been up to recently in my spooky life.

THE ANGEL EXPERIENCE LIVE

In 2010 I hit the stage. As the date of the show drew nearer I wondered what I had let myself in for. The event (a showcase of angel stories, meditations, songs, readings and aura photography) was performed by myself and several guest speakers; rather frustratingly, through no fault of my own, it coincided with my house move … and a week later my sister moved house, too.

The fabulous evening was organized by TV medium Tony Stockwell's production company and the team put an awful lot of work into preparing it. Unfortunately for me, the stress before the event was enormous, and I sheepishly admit I half-hoped that the organizers would cancel the event (nasty of me), but in the end I was delighted the production went ahead. It was a fantastic opportunity for me, and the audience seemed captivated. You always hope an event like this will be a roaring success, but when it happens it still comes as a shock (or perhaps that's just me!).

We finished the evening with the ABBA song 'I Have a Dream', which contains the immortal words, 'I believe in angels.' Actually I was horrified when it was suggested we end on a song – I can't sing a note and only agreed so long as we could get the audience to join in. Luckily they were happy to sing along and even waved their arms back and forth with the teeniest of encouragement from me – a useful distraction technique, I thought.

Unfortunately on the night my microphone picked up my voice a little better than I'd intended and my off-key voice rang out loud and clear. Thankfully the audience didn't seem to mind and no one complained at my terrible singing voice. I can turn my hand to a good many things, but singing is not one of them. Note to self: No more events which involve me singing!

All in all it was a hit – thank you, Tony!

A LITTLE GHOSTLY LOVE

A little off-track for me, this past year I also co-created a 'Ghost Workshop' CD with my lovely friend, TV medium Barrie John. We recorded at the home studio of our producer James and all went according to plan. Then, right at the end of the recording, we heard three loud knocks on the cupboard in the room. We were stunned and all looked at each other. Did that really happen? Surely that wasn't a real ghost?

The room next door belonged to James' daughter Holly, but Holly wasn't there at the time. No one else was even in the house – and anyway, the knocking definitely came from *inside* the room we were in. The knocking had even been picked up by our microphone, meaning we had to re-record our final few words because the knocking sound lay over the top of our final words. I suggested we leave the raps in the final recording, along with an explanation of what had happened, but James pointed out that no one would believe it was really ghosts … he was probably right!

BOOK-SIGNING ANGELS?

Among my book-signing events in 2010 was a very welcoming evening organized by The Chepstow Bookshop. Matt, the organizer, had a very impressive list of people attending further signing events later in the year, including many well-known names from TV, so I was excited to have been chosen for one of his well-attended gatherings. It's always such an honour when a bookshop invites you to speak.

The evening was made up of a talk by me, a question-and-answer session and then a book-signing. Many fans had travelled long distances, including a memorable group of women who call themselves 'The Angels'! The following day I received a thank-you e-mail from Matt, who told me, ' … really glad the event went so well. I was however rather shocked (and this is true) to find a large white feather when I was tidying my son's room the next morning.'

I guess Matt's angels were paying attention, too! How lovely for him to get his own confirmation that the angels were around. A white feather is a common sign that angels are with you, and Matt's angels were yelling loud and clear. I hope this means he'll invite me back again.

TELEPHONE FROM HEAVEN

Since my dad passed away nearly three years ago (at the time of writing), he's been a regular visitor from the other side. Many of you will be familiar with my writings about him, and my sister and I have even written a whole book about his afterlife adventures (due out November 2011)... details are on my website.

His antics are still continuing after all this time. My niece Jasmine won an award at college this year and my sister and her ex-husband attended the award ceremony. We all wanted to go but tickets were strictly limited, however I did wonder if my dad would be watching from heaven-side. I guess you don't need to buy a ticket if you're dead, as Dad later proved.

After the ceremony that night the family all met at my mother's house. My niece shyly showed off her award – but only when pressed by her excited aunts and uncles! Suddenly the light flickered in the room and someone suggested it might be Dad's spirit announcing his visit. Dad often flickered the lights when his name was mentioned or we were discussing important family things. Was this Dad now showing he was listening in on our conversation?

My sister Debbie, Jasmine's mum, jumped up immediately to share the experience that had happened to her earlier in the evening. The light flickering had reminded her. She told me, 'My mobile bleeped during the fashion show this evening and I looked down to see who had sent the message. After Dad died I kept his name and photograph in my mobile address book, but deleted the telephone number of course. I assumed that eventually someone else would be allocated the number …' she began.

By this time we were all paying attention to the story. 'Well when I opened up the phone case there was a little '1' next to Dad's picture to indicate that he had sent a message!'

Do the dead send telephone calls from heaven? It's not the first time I've heard of the phenomenon for sure. There was much rumbling of 'No way' and 'Really?' Now I guess the story would be even more dramatic if I were to tell you she clicked on the little box and there had been an actual message from the 'other side' (now how cool would that have been?). But no, there wasn't a message attached – how could there be? There was no telephone number programmed into the phone! But his message was the little '1' on the phone. He was saying, 'I'm here … I'm listening … I'm aware of what is going on.' Dad's timing, as always, was brilliant!

MOVING HOUSE ... AND THE PSYCHIC CAT

Moving from our Midlands home to our new place in Cornwall was a challenge to say the least; especially as I was particularly busy work-wise at the time. Just before we moved I'd been visited by the animal psychic Jackie Weaver. Jackie is working on a book about celebrity pets, and she came to do a psychic communication session with my cats Tigger and Magik. (Jackie is writing the book from the pets' point of view.) Now, I believe in all sorts of things, so I decided to be open-minded about this experience, even if it was a little out of my comfort zone. Jackie was soon to show me how good she is!

Settling down to 'chat' to my pets, she immediately started picking up on their personalities. She sensed their individual fears and preferences, and I was suitably impressed. Tigger likes the colour royal blue, she told me, and he'd like a cushion with tassels; strangely, I had always tied tassels on his bedding and had only recently taken them off. He'd always just looked like a posh cat who would appreciate such luxuries (and I enjoyed the fun of the decorating experience).

Jackie shared all sorts of little details ... about Tigger's life and mine. I always remember to tell the cats what I am doing and where I am going these days ... well, you never know, do you?!

Then Jackie dropped the bombshell: 'You won't be moving in September. Tigger says you'll move into your new house in October.' 'What?' We had been expecting the end of August or maybe the beginning of September. A move in October would have meant weeks of delays, so I chose to disbelieve this. Anyway, even if she could chat to my pets, was my cat psychic, too? How would my cat know the date of our house move, for goodness' sake? It seemed way too bizarre to consider. Yet Tigger knew more than we did ourselves.

Weeks passed and the inevitable delays occurred. We did indeed have many hold-ups with our moving date, and we finally left our old house on the last day of September and, just as Tigger had predicted, we moved into our new home on 1st October! Never underestimate the power of a psychic cat.

Our little black cat Magik also shared many insights on our life and hers, and afterwards Jackie arranged for her artist friend to do a cartoon-style painting of our 'famous' moggies. Cheers, Jackie (the new picture is hanging on my kitchen wall).

THE HOUSE MOVE AND HELP FROM HEAVEN?

Finding a house to move into was proving a difficult challenge, and after three trips (of nearly four hours' drive each time) we were getting desperate. We wanted to be in Cornwall, by the sea, an area we had been visiting for nearly 20 years. Like most people we had a very large 'wish list' for our new home. Working from home, John (my husband) and I needed an office each, and moving so far away from our family meant we had to have spare bedrooms, too. Top of the list was safety for the cats, so I needed a quiet location for their protection and to give me the peace and quiet I wanted so that I could write my books and articles.

We'd found one perfect house on each visit, but due to various delays had lost them both. In the end I was getting desperate and turned skywards. 'Dad, please can you help me find the perfect house?' And I just kept my fingers crossed.

When we saw the details of one particular house, it didn't immediately jump out. Clearly it hadn't appealed to anyone else, either, as no one else had been to see it. From the photograph the building looked dark and old-fashioned. The rooms were empty in each image, and didn't photograph well, and the proximity to the local town made it an unlikely prospect – but something made us book a viewing just the same.

When we pulled up outside, I began to get excited. The house wasn't dark but shaded by beautiful mature trees surrounding it. It may have been close to town but it was down a private tree-lined drive off a quiet road ... convenient and secluded. Once we stepped inside, we could see that the rooms were bright and large. The only sound I could hear was birdsong. YES! The poor photographs had been heaven-sent: they had kept away other house-hunters, which was clearly to our advantage.

A few short days later we knew the house was ours ... was it a coincidence that we heard the news on Dad's birthday? Maybe ... On moving day we followed a large van into town, and it had the word DAD on the back (I guess the initials for a local company), and waiting for us at the front door was a large white feather (the angels' calling-card) stuck in the doormat ... in fact it was still there, several weeks later. I like to think that Dad may have had a little hand in the house-moving process, and thank goodness for that! Actually we regularly have white feathers stuck to the doormat and I choose to believe they are all angel signs.

My life is strange compared to many people's; my day-to-day existence is tinged with paranormal encounters, yet I often wonder, is it because I choose to open my eyes to the magic that is all around me? You can, too ... simply read on and I'll share some more magic with you.

Are angels real? You'll want to examine the evidence with me ...

PS My daughter did indeed have a healthy baby girl the following New Year's Day, 1st January 2011, and loads of people all over the world wrote to remind me about the magic of the numbers 1:1:11 (a spiritual awakening).

Welcome to my spooky life!

An Angel Saved My Life

In three words I can sum up everything
I've learned about life: it goes on.
– Robert Frost

It was a great many years ago now that I heard angel music for the first and last time. The angelic choir sound was coming from my bathroom at home, where my young daughter was sleeping on the floor. The poor thing had caught a tummy-bug and had been sick for many hours ... although I know as an adult she won't want me to keep going on about this now. The point of the story was that I'd asked the angels earlier on in the evening if they could help. I needed healing for Georgina and peace for me (selfish of me, I know).

You'd think, wouldn't you, that angels would have more important things to do, like watch over areas of the world suffering famine or wars? But I realized then, and I've carried the thought with me ever since, that angels are everywhere and all of our life's problems are important to them, too. No matter what the issue, no matter how small our concerns, the angels are there in the background supporting us in whatever way they can.

This particular instance was one of my more dramatic experiences. The sound of harps and harmonies was filtering out through the door of the bathroom and, of course, when I went to explore there was no one there ... no one that I could see. My daughter was sleeping peacefully on the floor, wrapped up in a bundle of towels. I left her there to rest and in the morning when she awoke she was well again.

I've longed for dramatic angel encounters like this ever since, and although they occur from time to time, as a human being it never seems to be enough for me! What do the angels need to do to ensure that we believe in them? What do they have to do so that we know they are with us?

Do angels exist? You bet they do! I've spent a great many years of my life exploring the phenomenon of angel experiences and I can tell you without a shadow of a doubt ... they're real! If you're still waiting for an angel encounter, maybe you too have to ask yourself ... have I had one already? Have I ignored this miraculous encounter? Surprisingly, many do.

Angels, beings of light, winged ones – whatever you want to call them, they are watching over us and taking care of us. They are our guides and guardians, our loving saviours ... our guardian angels, in fact! And they assist us in our life's journey, and comfort and heal us along the way. I love angels!

WANT A LITTLE INSPIRATION?

Angels feature in every area of my life. I call on them when I'm sad and lonely and I use their images to decorate my home; although my husband thinks I go a little overboard with angels on everything, I believe you can never have too many angels in your life. But that's just me! The figurines and angel paintings represent the real angels to me. Their presence in my home means I think about them a lot of the time. Every time I turn a corner there's another angel. You can bring angels into your own life like this, too. Maybe yours will be a little more subtle than mine!

Working with angels means requesting their company, and because angels surround me in a physical sense, by the use of imagery it's not hard to remember to invite them into my world. I ask angels to bless my food, help with my writing and heal my body when I am asleep. How can the angels help you today?

Looking up at the wall above my desk, I spot my new angel clock, an angel globe on the shelf, an angel calendar, angel bumper stickers and an angel perching over the edge of a dish containing angel affirmation cards! Even the photograph albums and address books which sit on the side of the desk are decorated with glittery angels, and as I've already mentioned, my drink coasters contain pink and purple angels which match my clock (yes, honestly!). I bring you these lists to inspire you. Do you have angels in your home? Angels sit on the edge of shelves and carry photographs. I have angels on my candle holders and angels on my candles. Even my orchid plant is decorated with the image of one of the angel-cherubs from the Sistine Chapel (the chapel in the Apostolic Palace: the official residence of the Pope in Vatican City which is famous for its architecture, art and decoration, particularly of angels). I love to browse around gift shops for more little angels, and friends often surprise me with wonderful angel gifts – most recently a pair of delightful knitted angels, an angel on a peg, angel stickers, jewellery and angel bookmarks.

I have posted some of my collection on my Facebook page if you're interested in having a look – I change it from time to time. Angel plaques hang on the wall in my writing room and angel wind-chimes and feather wings hang from an angel-decorated pine cupboard with a glass front. Just when I think I have collected everything that exists, friends or fans buy me more. I especially love the plain white, cream and gold angels of every size and description – the gold ones are especially decadent, don't you think?

If you want to bring angels into your life, then maybe a little collection of your own is a great place to start? You don't have to buy expensive pieces – maybe you could have a go at creating your own artwork or crafts! What fun! As we speak, Alan, an angel artist, is designing me some personalized angel cards (you can check out his work at www.cloughart.com).

Want more inspiration? I often print angel-decorated stationery from my computer, or use angel notelets. I have a gold stamp pad and stamp on an angel feather design, or choose one of several angel cut-outs to hand print an angel onto my envelopes – and, of course, I fill my envelopes with angel confetti!

WORKING WITH YOUR GUARDIAN ANGEL

Not only are angels real but we all have our very own guardian angel: a being who has been with us since the very beginning of time … our time, our life. Your own guardian angel is always by your side. Know it's true, feel it deep inside of yourself; let this knowledge comfort you.

Angels protect and guard us, but mainly they love us. Feel this love from your angel. The unconditional love your angel brings is unlike any other you experience as a human being. The greatest love you've ever experienced feels nothing like as strong as the amazing and all-powerful love from your guardian. Let this love from your angel into your life and let it flow into your heart.

Everyone without exception has their own angel ... even if you are not a perfect human being (and hey, who is?). We all make mistakes, it's part of being human and it's the reason we are here on Earth at this time. We are born to learn and to grow. So many of us criticize ourselves every day – do you have that inner critic, the one who nags away at you all day long telling you off? Does that voice say, 'You're useless, you're rubbish, you can't do it, you'll never make it ...'? Yes, most of us do, but our angels are NOT that voice.

Many of the stories in this book deal with healing experiences. Having inner confidence helps with your emotional wellbeing. If you believe in yourself, know and trust your own choices, then you feel better about the world and yourself in it.

LET THE LOVE FLOW

Your angels want you only to love yourself as they love you. Can you try? Each time you hear a negative voice in your head, replace it with a new one. Say, 'I love you', 'You are doing a great job', 'Well done me!' The changes in the planet right now mean we all have to raise our inner vibrations. Think positive and loving thoughts. Even your private inner judgements count. Try and watch what you think as well as what you say ... it's not easy, so start with yourself first of all. Love begins at HOME; right in your own heart. How can others love us if we fail to love ourselves?

Angels are everywhere right now. Can you feel your angel right there by your side? They want to reassure us, care for us and, especially, love us. They can intervene in our lives in simple ways or get involved in the more dramatic things that happen to us. I especially love when they intervene in a life-saving way. Their involvement during life-threatening times can be the difference between life and death, and if it's 'not your time …' they seem able to literally pluck you from danger. Don't take silly risks with this, though … it's not a game. If you throw yourself in front of a bus on purpose, expect to get run over.

Angels are beautiful creatures, but it's not so much how they look as how they make us feel that counts. Encounter an angel and you will immediately feel calm and peaceful (though admittedly you might initially be startled, too!). Angels are majestic beings. Seeing one with your physical eyes is pretty awe-inspiring! Being in the presence of an angel will change your life forever, and more and more of us around the world are having angel experiences of all sorts. Feeling, sensing or touching an angel is a healing experience.

Angel energy is magical and therapeutic; in fact, therapists all over the world ask angels to be present during their healing sessions, with good reason. Working with the angels is like plugging in a lamp … everything is brighter, lighter and warmer. If you work with healing, call on the Archangel Raphael – the healing angel – for a little specialized assistance.

HOW YOU MIGHT EXPERIENCE AN ANGEL IN YOUR LIFE

- An angel might bring you the gift of a white feather or a small coin.
- You might sense an angel around you – you can just feel that they are with you. Something about the energy around you changes or you feel tingly.

- Maybe you will be lucky enough to hear angel music (breathtaking choir-like harmonies ... the sound of a harp, just as traditional ideas of the angels suggest!)

- Perhaps for you the angel will appear on a cloud of perfume: delightful scents of exotic flowers is a common sign.

- Perhaps you will catch one in a photograph: glowing balls of light or wispy cloud-like formations which appear behind your loved ones, especially on special occasions. Angels in dreams always have that wonderful glow about them.

- Maybe you'll hear an angel voice: angels often warn humans of danger with a few simple words and phrases like 'Stop' or simply 'Slow down' ... our deceased loved ones can do this, too.

- Sometimes in times of distress an angel will hold your hand or rest a hand on your shoulder – you'll actually feel this sensation as if it were happening to you in a physical way. It will feel so real you'll find yourself opening your eyes or looking around to see who is comforting you.

- Angels occasionally wake people in the night: it might be because you are in danger or simply that your dream-state higher vibration makes it easier for the angels to visit you at this time. Your angel may stand at the bottom of the bed or by your side. Sometimes they appear to sit on the bed and you'll feel the mattress sink down just a little bit.

Of course angels appear to people in many ways; these are just a few. Perhaps you've already had an angel encounter? If you haven't, let's have one right now:

An Exercise to Help You Feel Close to Your Angel

After you've read through this once, close your eyes – yes, right that very minute. Relax … in fact, spend a few moments relaxing, and then I want you to use your imagination. Imagination is the key to reaching your inner world, so I want you to 'see' in your mind's eye (visually inside your head) your angel standing in front of you. What does your angel look like? Is it male or female? What colour hair does your angel have? What colour eyes? Look closely right now. What is your angel wearing … does he or she have wings or a halo? I want you to see every detail and then write down what you have seen … do this immediately before you read any further – it won't take you long!

Working with your angel takes just a teeny bit of effort on your part! If you can't 'see' these things, ask yourself, 'If I did know, what would the answer to these questions be?' Then write that down. Use your intuition to guide your answers … just write!

Right, once you've written this down, close your eyes again. Ask your angel, 'What is your name?' What do you hear? If you hear nothing ask again – know that there is an answer to your question … and just write it down.

Sometimes an angel won't have a name as we understand it. Your angel is known by their skills, thoughts and feelings, which are interpreted by others in a visual or vibrational way, by the colours and light that they exhibit from their glowing angel forms.

Therefore, your angel may suggest that you give him or her a name.

> Give yourself permission to do this. Name your angel!
> Choose a favourite name right this very second – or
> simply make a name up … go for it! You angel's name is
> whatever you want it to be! Now open your eyes again
> and write this down … yes, do it now before you forget!

If you want to work with your angels in this way then take the time to have a pen to hand! I usually suggest you buy a special notebook for writing your angel notes. It's lovely to do these things by hand, but you can also type them up in a special file. At first, just get started – just write!

> OK, now close your eyes again … make sure you are
> really relaxed this time and take a few moments to do
> this. This time your angel is stepping forward (with your
> permission) to hold you in a loving embrace. Feel your
> angel's gift of pure, unconditional love … know you are
> surrounded by this love at all times. Really relax into the
> exercise at this time and really feel the energies that come
> from holding your guardian angel. Don't rush away, enjoy
> the experience.

> Your angel is always with you, caring for you, loving
> you and protecting you. You never have to face anything
> alone. Know this deep within your heart. It will give you
> confidence as you go about your day-to-day life. Only
> when you have fully explored this experience, move on
> to the next part of the exercise.

Now ask your angel for healing: healing for your body and healing for your soul. Relax as your angel brings you healing energy. I want you to feel the energy surround your body and sink down into the places where you really need it. We carry our troubles in our shoulders and lower backs in particular. I often get pains behind my eyes when I am worried or stressed and, strangely, at the tops of my arms as if I'm carrying my troubles, literally. Search out your bodily aches and ask the angels to heal these areas, too. Spend a few minutes 'imagining' this happening, then when you are ready open your eyes and makes notes of anything that happened.

Ask your angel for a message or a mantra (a positive statement you can repeat throughout the day) ... then just listen. Here are some examples:

- *I am happy and well.*
- *I am filled with divine light.*
- *The abundance of the universe always comes easily to me.*
- *I have many friends.*
- *A new job will come easily to me.*

Your message may come as words or a feeling. Then thank your angel, open your eyes and write down everything you remember. Make a note of this page of the book and come back to it as often as you like. Get into a bit of a routine and maybe do this every day for a few weeks. Make a note of any changes that happen as you do so.

In this next story my reader felt her loved one hug her. It's a magical, healing experience to have a deceased relative or friend do this. For a brief moment your loved one becomes your guardian angel ... it's when you know they are still around you. Can your angel hold your hand? You bet they can!

My 'Angel' Hugged Me

My mum passed away on 14th June 2010 with a long-term illness. We were very close and she was like my best friend, my confidante and my advisor ... she was everything to me. After the funeral I felt Mum's presence a few times; once she was beside my bed during the night, which I found very comforting.

I missed her so much and after a couple of months I was really low and cried and prayed to God to just let Mum come to me one more time. One night my mum did come to me. It felt completely real. She looked so happy and she was smiling; her face seemed to be lit up and she looked radiant. Although Mum had worn oxygen tubes while she'd been unwell, she didn't have her oxygen tubes on as she passed away. Of course you worry about how they will be if they do appear, but she made a point of telling me, 'Pamela, look, I'm OK.' She didn't seem to move her mouth; it was as if she were talking to me through my mind.

Next Mum hugged me and I was crying as I felt her arms around me as she hugged me. I felt so warm and at total peace; it was amazing and totally real. In the morning I awoke feeling overwhelmed with warmth, peace and love. I truly believe she came to visit me when I needed it the most, and I will never forget that night for the rest of my life.

Before Mum passed we had a holiday booked, and before she passed away she said to me, 'Pamela, after all of this you will need your holiday.' She was so right, so I still went on the holiday and tried to enjoy the experience as best as I could.

One particular night we were having a really lovely meal with some friends and we were talking about my mum while we ate. I can remember feeling quite settled that evening. It was the best I'd felt since losing Mum. After returning home I did feel it was time to get back to work. I'm a nurse and I felt it was important to continue to care for others and to enjoy my life for my mum. My husband put the holiday photos on the computer and when we looked at them my 14-year-old daughter said, 'Mum there are some "orbs" around your head.' I didn't know what she was talking about and looked closely at the photographs taken the night of the meal. There were three distinct circles of light, and we believe it was Mum, my nan and my granddad all joining us on holiday. Strangely enough, before we went away I did pray to God for a sign that Mum was with her parents and was being cared for. I believe this was my sign: my beautiful mum trying to tell me that all is well.

I haven't felt able to discuss my experiences with the rest of my family because they are not very spiritual ... and will think I've gone mad! But I have shared my story with a couple of close friends who think it truly is Mum bringing her gift of love.

Even though I miss Mum terribly, I get great comfort in the messages from heaven and look forward to many more. When Mum wants to visit me I'll always be open to her call. My outlook on life and the afterlife has really made me a more spiritual person. I will never fear death because I know when my time comes my beautiful mum, my nan and my granddad will come for me, and for Dad when his time comes, and will greet us with open arms.

Pam, England

Did you spot the special point where Pam's mum was reassuring her that she was well? That is so important to the grieving. Isn't it wonderful that she actually felt her mother's touch in a physical way? My dad did this for two of my sisters when he visited in dreams and danced with them as he had done in life. Both sisters explained that they felt the touch as if he were alive. It felt real. It really does happen that way. I love that they also had beautiful orbs on the image (beautiful balls of light which appear on photographs and which some people believe might be signs of spirit or angels).

Pam's mum also communicated using telepathy ... that is the usual way for spirits to contact us. Spirits don't have normal physical bodies in the way that we understand them, therefore voice boxes are also unnecessary. All communication in heaven is done through telepathy (mind-to-mind contact in words, pictures or thought-patterns) or through the use of symbolism (the same way in which we receive messages from our higher selves, angels and guides during dreams).

WHAT DO ANGELS LOOK LIKE?

Sometimes people remember being awake during their angel encounters; others are asleep but aware, and yet others are convinced they are unconscious ... but still remember their angel visitations. Some angels take on human-like appearances, others are large and shining beings; some are tall and some are very small, like faeries. Some folk share encounters with wisps of cloud-like beings, yet others see twinkling lights or orbs of glowing radiance in all different colours which glow in the dark like searchlights. In the following stories I'll share all of these and many other variations. How would you like an angel to visit you?

Have you had an angel encounter? Is your angel a being of light, a deceased loved one or an unknown spirit or guide of some sort? Maybe your angel is a being from other realms or dimensions ... Let's explore some of this a little more. I've collected some wonderful real-life angel stories to inspire and amaze you. Let me reassure you ... every story in this book is a true experience sent to me by my lovely readers from all over the world. It happened to them, and it can happen to you, too.

The Voice That Saved My Life

Last September my husband and I both started to feel very unwell at the same time. We were both suffering from headaches and extreme tiredness, and as the week went on we were both starting to have dizzy spells, too. Even our poor little hamster 'Charlie' seemed very grumpy, although we didn't put all of this together and we had no idea what was wrong with us.

Then one Monday morning I was sat on the settee before leaving for work and I felt awful, so unwell. I decided to see if I could call on any 'otherworldly' assistant and started asking any 'beings' that might be around at the time what was wrong with us and why were we ill. I suddenly became aware of an elderly spirit gentleman in the room. I didn't know this man and strangely I wasn't frightened even though he was sitting next to me! He looked at me and clearly said to me, 'It's carbon monoxide, get it sorted!' I was stunned.

I can still hear those six words so clearly, even now after all this time. I immediately shot onto the computer and looked it up. The phrase 'carbon monoxide poisoning' was right there on the internet, and sure enough the symptoms were an exact match to those we were experiencing! I immediately phoned our GP who said he was so pleased that we had recognized the symptoms, as people rarely do. I didn't tell him how I'd got to know, though!

The GP told me to go immediately to the Accident and Emergency Department at the local hospital. To be honest that turned out to be a waste of time because they kept me waiting for the best part of four hours, then told me I was fine and sent me home, even though my blood pressure was extremely high!

Of course we still had the carbon monoxide problem to deal with, so I called out a gas engineer and asked him to see if he could discover the cause of the problem. The engineer looked at our boiler and immediately disconnected it and served us a warning order not to use it again. He condemned it due to the carbon monoxide emissions! Surprise, surprise!

I dread to think about what would have happened to us if that lovely spirit gentleman had not told me what it was. My husband and I and our little hamster might not be here today! We are so lucky to be protected by the angels. I feel so blessed.

I've decided to dedicate my life to working with these beautiful beings, and I feel so fortunate that I've been able to see and hear them. They have literally saved my life.

Caroline, England

Isn't this story amazing?! I know most people would have been too scared of seeing the spirit and not hung around long enough to hear what he had to say. I wonder who he was. As Caroline didn't recognize him he clearly wasn't a relative of hers. Maybe he was someone who had lived in the house a long time ago, or perhaps he was just Caroline's guardian angel? All we do know is that he acted as her guardian angel when he was needed the most. Let's hope the rest of us are just as lucky. More of these stories later.

BEING YOUR OWN ANGEL

Don't forget, you can be your own guardian angel here ... ask your gas supplier to let you have carbon monoxide detectors to place around your own home (also available in many home maintenance or DIY shops). Make sure you have several around the house, particularly by your cooker and gas fires as well as on the boiler itself. These plastic disks with a special insert are not much bigger than a stamp and aren't very expensive. The material is sensitive to the gas and will change colour if emissions are detected. They need changing regularly, though, so don't forget to make a note of the date on the special strip provided. This is your angel warning from me, so get it done! Why not keep one in your suitcase for when you travel away from home? Holiday apartments can be dangerous, too!

Another thing that angels have warned about in the past is smoke detectors. Do you have these in your home? In some areas the local fire station supply them for free, and if your home is rented your landlord may have to provide these (check your rental agreement). Test them regularly and check the batteries (always keep spares). Check your alarms today ... before you go to bed, and make a note in your diary to check yours regularly (at least once a week). If you always check on the same day each week, you are unlikely to forget.

THE ROLE OF OUR ANGELS

Have you ever been aware of a spirit presence in your life? Many people feel they are being helped by an unseen guide or guardian during their time of greatest need. I believe this is when our angels draw closer to us. What better time for the angels to make themselves known to us than when we need their presence the most? Yet your guardian angel is always with you really. We are never abandoned by our guardian angels and spiritual guides; even if you've never felt their company.

Emotion seems to play a part. I know there have been times when I've been quite cross with my own angels: where are they and why aren't they helping me, I wonder. Actually I get quite rude with them … but it's me that's wrong. Angels should be treated with the same politeness you would offer to a fellow human being. Maybe I'm just grumpy? I'm not sure rudeness makes them any more likely to appear.

Angels can't interfere in our lives but are always close when we need their help. Some people (especially me) forget this and occasionally ask the angels to do silly and pointless things … especially if it's something I might just as easily do myself. Humans are here to learn things for themselves; and regular readers will have heard me say this before: sometimes we are better left to work things out for ourselves (it's certainly more satisfying!).

Have you ever asked your angels to bring you the winning lottery numbers, or asked to win at the bingo? I think most people do this, we all think that a large sum of money will solve all of our problems – yet people with lots of money aren't necessarily any happier than those without! Of course, the more money we have the more we want! Money can bring us choices but often it just gets in the way. Surveys on the happiest people often indicate that those with simple lives and less 'stuff' are those who feel the most contented. Expensive belongings bring problems of their own: you have to take care of them, insure them, guard them, etc. Be rich with family, be rich with friends, be content with Nature and be happy and grateful for the comforts in your life ... like your bed or the fact that you have enough food to eat. Not everyone has these things.

Angels can help with many purposes, and although they can help us find the money to pay the bills, money isn't really their speciality! Some of us are guilty of asking our angels to help with everything (yes, sorry, that's been me again)! Yet we do need to work out some problems for ourselves! Imagine if we carried a normal and healthy child around until he was ten years old because we wanted to protect him from the danger of learning to walk ... or falling over! It sounds ridiculous, doesn't it? Angels don't carry us ... not when the answer to the problem is within grasping distance, at least. *Carrying* is saved for life-threatening moments, not normal 'not sure what to do next' times.

Look ... don't feel bad about asking angels for help, though. Sometimes tasks can be a little too challenging, and angels *are* great at easing our burdens just a little bit ... usually by bringing in human helpers to lighten the load. Placing the right person in front of you is probably the most helpful they can be.

Often it's human helpers we need. Who are the human helpers in your life? When have people helped you when you have been in trouble? Can you recall a time when a school mate stuck up for you in class or a young child whispered exactly the simple words you needed to hear? Maybe your most profound comfort came from a stranger or a pet? Maybe an animal or bird hopped into view to distract you momentarily from your problems? (I had a robin do this for me just yesterday.) Have you been an angel today? Don't ignore cries for help from the people around you ... an angel may just have placed YOU in their path for a reason. Perhaps today YOU are the angel?

This next angel experience is one of the more dramatic that I've had in my postbag. Who gave this verbal warning and saved three lives?

Saved from a Terrible Fate

Years ago, way back in 1989, my former husband and I were living on and managing a dry-stock farm in New Zealand. It was late springtime and we'd had a long stretch of wet weather. One of the back paddocks, and one we set aside for hay each year, had a large natural pond, which had formed many years previously. The owner had decided it should be drained, because each year the Paradise Shelducks would arrive around the pond and, as they are grass-eaters, would eat more and more of the grass set aside for hay each year, making our job of ensuring there was enough hay for the winter stock feed a really tough task.

In previous years we had tried deterrents, using the boom guns from the DOC (Department of Conservation) and they had not worked for us: the ducks, lovely as they are, just kept coming. As Paradise Shelduck is a protected species, we could not cull them, either.

The owner's son, who was our resident mechanic and did a lot of the seasonal work with the heavy machinery, was asked to come and have a look at the pond and discuss which would be the best way to drain it. As both my husband and I worked the property, we all went down to the paddock together to check out the pond. Off from the side of the pond was a shallow indent in the ground which formed a natural overflow drain for the excess water to run off; it led the gully down into the river below.

All three of us walked out to the bluff, but not near the edge ... we all stayed back from the edge by about 10 feet to make sure we stayed well out of danger. While the men discussed the best way to do the job, I just listened.

The day was lovely, warm and sunny, and after all the rain we'd had it made a really nice change. Suddenly I felt a massive force around me and I heard someone yell, 'RUN!' In an instant all three of us bolted without hesitating, and just where we had been standing the bluff just caved away into the gully below. My husband just looked at me ... and the boss' son asked me how I knew that it was going to cave in. Apparently I had been the one to shout RUN ... but why? I had only heard it in my head!

All I remembered was looking at the men, and in a split second we were running and I hadn't known why. I believe an angel was with us that day and saved us from a terrible fate ...

Susanne, Australia

Has Susanne been the psychic one of the group? Had the angels perhaps chosen her as the one most likely to take action that warm day? Why did she feel the force around her and what exactly was it? These experiences often leave more questions than they answer, and these answers we'll probably never discover ... not on this side of life, anyway. It was clearly not their 'time'!

Have you ever had life-saving angel experiences yourself? Has an angel ever saved your life in a dramatic way? Strangely, many people forget these experiences after they happen. The brain can't understand it so buries the experience deep in the back of the mind. You might only remember your own angel encounters while reading others' in this book.

Angels and spirits are everywhere ... let's discover a little more ...

Spirit in the Workplace

Science can only determine what is, but not what shall be, and beyond its realm, value judgements remain indispensable.
– **Albert Einstein**

To explore the belief in angels we need to look at life, but to appreciate life we need also to consider death. Death is a funny old thing ... not funny ha-ha but funny peculiar; although I'll be honest, even though death is not something we usually laugh about, there are plenty of 'dead' jokes to be found on the internet! Maybe for some of us death is something we ponder ... a lot. I know that as I get older I consider it more ... perhaps it's not fear of death we carry but fear of dying? What happens when we die? Where do we go? Will we ever see our loved ones again? Do we all become ghosts?

It's common for spirits to visit houses they loved when they were alive as well as the people who live there, but some spirits are interested in visiting their old businesses or places of work. Many more spirits are seen in the place where they passed over:

this might be at their place of work anyway (it happens, sadly) or perhaps the deceased died in hospital. That means that spirits are everywhere …

DEAD … BUT ALIVE

People are brought back from the very brink of death all the time and all over the world. The lines of life and death have blurred over the years. The human body craves life, and people survive extraordinary trauma, illnesses and accidents. These days we have many tests to show when a person has completely expired, but it wasn't always that way. The body of Matthew Wall was being lifted into his grave back in the early sixteenth century when one of the pallbearers tripped up, causing Matthew to awaken from his unconscious state. Wall lived for quite a few more years, finally dying for real in 1595. He is said to have celebrated his 'awakening' every year!

A more tragic incident happened in 1984 in New York. During a post-mortem the 'corpse' suddenly jumped up and grabbed the examiner by the throat just as he was making his first cut. Sadly the pathologist died of shock after the incident, even though the 'corpse' lived a long and happy life.

A happier story was the death … and life of the Reverend Schwartz. The reverend was lying in his coffin at his funeral when he 'came to' listening to the sound of his favourite hymn. Luckily the coffin was still open when the reverend suddenly sat up and asked the mourners why they were all looking at him!

JUST IN CASE …

Many death-customs, of years gone by, grew out of a fear of being buried alive. This was much more likely to happen in ancient times. Advances in medical science mean this is most unlikely to happen these days ... thankfully!

In many cultures people would sometimes 'wake' the deceased. 'Waking' was the practice of sitting by the bedside with the corpse until burial in case the deceased was revived in the meantime. This is related to the Catholic ritual of the wake, where the body is displayed in its coffin for three days before burial. Some people specified in their Wills that they wished certain procedures to be performed on their bodies to ensure they were really dead. Others insisted on being buried with knives or guns in case they woke up after being buried ... and wanted to finish the job themselves! I've read of coffins being specifically created in Belgium and the United States which included bells and flags ... even with a lamp which would light if signs of life were indicated in the coffin!

Mary Baker Eddy, the founder of the Christian Science movement, was said to have been interred with a working telephone. Whether this is true or simply rumour is difficult to ascertain. Even in more recent times these types of facilities appear from time to time. Right up to 1995 you could acquire an Italian-designed casket complete with bleepers, microphones and two-way speakers. The kit also included a torch and an oxygen tank, just in case! I imagine these days that people would prefer to have their mobile phone and perhaps a charger ... just in case.

DEATH RITUALS

Many traditional death rituals are well documented. A sacred rite in Hinduism is *Niravapanjali*, where the ashes of the deceased are immersed in holy water, enabling the soul to rise to the heavenly realms. Rituals vary from country to country according to traditional beliefs about what happens after someone dies. Even crying, which is spontaneous in Western countries, is considered mandatory (on occasion) to show the loss and love connection between loved ones in some funeral services at different places around the world.

Around most of Europe and America the body is 'dressed' for burial, usually in favourite clothes or ceremonial outfits worn in life, as a sign of the greatest of respect for the deceased. Grooming is part of this procedure and includes hair brushing and make-up – even for men. Embalming, a procedure performed to stall decomposition of the body so that it is suitable for public viewing, is common. Other traditions see death as just the beginning of another life. In some areas of Africa a corpse is prepared for this long journey by bathing and dressing it appropriately.

Jesus' resurrection took place on the third day after his death, according to the Bible. Maybe this is the reason that the deceased remains unburied for three days or more in many customs? Some customs hold that the deceased can still hear everything that is said about them during this short period of time. My postbag seems to indicate that our loved ones are aware of many things that happen to us (although perhaps not everything), and like to 'come back' and let us know! Other cultures bury coins with the deceased to 'pay the ferryman' for their crossing or pay their way once they arrive in heaven; these might be placed in the pocket, on the eyes or even in the mouth! In Russia the coin would be thrown into the grave to help the deceased acquire a better position in the afterlife.

After my father passed over, the funeral director asked us if we wanted to leave any items in the coffin; it came as a welcome relief to the proceedings as we listed all sorts of objects which represented his life, suitable for burial alongside this special man … some of them were funny. His cigarettes (not our favourite of items), mints (which he always ate to disguise the smell of the cigarettes which he'd 'given up'), his fishing rod, his walking stick, his dancing shoes, his wallet … logic becoming completely obsolete as we looked at the symbols of his existence, a short moment of fun in an otherwise very sad time!

Some of the stories in earlier postbags have included dream-visits from surviving family members who've been shown the burial clothes of the dead in a dream even though they were not aware of what these items were (perhaps because they had been unable to attend the funeral). These experiences indicate good proof of afterlife visitation to me.

The Mexicans have a fabulous ritual called 'Day of the Dead' (*Dia de los Muertos*) which is celebrated on 2nd November (also known as All Souls Day, the day that follows All Saints Day/ All Hallows Day, which is of course the day after 31st October, Halloween). Living relatives remember their deceased friends and family on this day. Many homes create an altar which contains photographs of the deceased (the ancestors), along with candles, food and flowers … particularly marigolds, which are known as *flor de muerto* or flower of the dead. Candies and sweets decorated in the shape of skulls and skeletons are common! The belief is that one day the dead will return to be with the living; the Day of the Dead ensures that the ancestors are never forgotten.

I love these rituals and I think it would be helpful to celebrate the life of a loved one by creating rituals of our own. Rather than visit a graveside daily (which stops the living carrying on with their own lives) imagine a family get-together once a year (or once every couple of years or so) to celebrate passed-over loved ones. This is a wonderful opportunity for sharing photographs and positive stories of their lives.

I'd also suggest memorializing loved ones in some way: create a website, write a poem, create a scrapbook, etc. You can also leave a living legacy by starting a charity to raise funds for something close to the heart of the deceased, or have a coffee morning or run a race to raise money for a favourite cause. All these things help the grieving process. Your loved one will be aware of your actions from across the heavens.

THE SPIRIT RETURNS

Life and death are a natural part of existence in a hospital. It makes sense that spirits would frequent places of healing: watching over the birth of newborn relatives, caring for sick loved ones and holding the hands of the dying ... and all from the other side of life. We are cared for this side of life and beyond. Your loved ones still show concern when you are sick and will do whatever they can to assist in healing and comforting ... all from the afterlife.

In these next stories some of the spirit visitors are ex-patients, some may well be ex-staff who worked in the hospital many years ago; others are either angels or deceased loved ones either assisting in the care of the patients or helping them to cross over to the other side of life. This first story has been sent to me by a nurse ... I'm not sure, still, if it was a helpful angel ... or a helpful ghost! Perhaps it doesn't even matter.

Hello? Is it Me You're Looking for?

Many years ago I was working as a nurse doing the night shift on a ward I wasn't familiar with. When it came to break-time, one of the nurses made up a bed for us in the treatment room. I went on the first break and the other nurse told me she would give me a knock when it was time to go back on duty. That sounded fine, so I settled down for a rest.

I'd been asleep for a while when I was suddenly woken by the sound of a light tapping on the door and a very quiet voice saying, 'Hello?'

It didn't seem long since I'd fallen asleep and I was really tired, so to be honest I decided to pretend I hadn't heard the knocking. I just turned over to go back to sleep, and a couple of minutes later the same thing happened; again I ignored it even though I knew I should really go back to work. The third time it happened I ignored it again and this time the door opened, and footsteps walked across the room and stopped by the bed. I looked up and no one was there! Spooky, huh?

When I did go back on duty I didn't tell anyone else what had happened because I thought they'd be too scared to sleep in the room. The hospital has since been demolished to make way for a housing estate but apparently it used to be the old workhouse. Not surprisingly, I had many other spooky experiences while I was working there.

Trudie, England

Some people believe that ghosts are a sort of 'echo' from the past. It's possible that their life-force energy is 'recorded' on the atmosphere somehow like a voice on magnetic tape. At least this invisible visitor seemed friendly enough. This next story involves a visible visitor, but who was it? The difference in this case is that the nurse not only *saw* the person, she even spoke to her. Could this have been a human being in the wrong place, a case of mistaken identity, a mistake on the part of the nurse or perhaps a spirit visitor? What do you think? Was it an angel?

The Visitor

My Dad is 82 years old and on 8th April 2010 he went into the hospital to have a prostate operation. I took my mum to be with him, and my son and nephew were at the hospital both before and after his operation. I told Dad we would pray for him, which I did. Mum said she was also praying while we waited in the motel room.

After the operation we all returned to Dad's room and the young nurse said, rather bizarrely we thought, 'The other one must have gone to the cafeteria.' We had no idea what she meant because we'd all been together, so we asked her whom she was talking about. The nurse explained that she had spoken to an older woman who'd sat on a chair in the corner of Dad's room when we were away. She waited there while Dad was having his operation. The nurse got a good look at her and described her as someone with blonde bobbed hair, large reading glasses and a hearing aid. The nurse even spoke to the woman and told her that she could wait in the cafeteria while Dad was having the operation and that when he came back from theatre they would phone her.

My son, nephew and I were confused because we didn't know anyone who even fitted that description, and we never did find out who it was. We do have a suspicion, though. I believe it was an angel and she was telling us that everything was going to be OK. I like to think she was reassuring us that Dad was being taken care of.

Bronwyn, Australia

I love a story with a bit of mystery! Whether human or angel, this woman still brought comfort to the family! Maybe it was a deceased relative, or Bronwyn's dad's guardian angel in disguise! This next story is fascinating ... it's filled with love from the angels and a little extra feathery gift. I love angel feathers; they are the perfect sign that an angel is watching over you.

The Gift of Loving Angels

Penelope (a colleague who works in the same classroom as me) confided that since her husband died three years ago, she had received a white feather as an angel gift on several occasions, particularly when she was feeling really down. She often shared details of her belief in angels.

We hadn't talked about angels for several weeks when she mentioned to me (in our empty classroom, the children having left for the day) that she was going to send some 'angel wishes' to a widowed friend in need, via text message.

I then said to her, 'You know, Penelope, the only experience I've ever had of angels was when I had a facial in Bulgaria two years ago; I must have been in a very relaxed state, as I felt myself start to 'drift off' – but actually I think it was the opposite: I became very aware at the point I became very relaxed. At this point the beauty therapist woman had left the room and I think she left me for about half an hour. Actually, I don't know for how long, but it seemed like a long time. As soon as she disappeared I experienced angels who came and knelt either side of me and at the end of the bed. There were seven angels altogether.

They had the traditional wings, like we see in paintings, and were not looking at me full on but just looking across to each other. I didn't really see their faces but they seemed to be wearing red. I was surprised because usually when you see pictures of angels they are wearing white. I remember at the time thinking, 'Is this what it's like when you die?' But somehow I knew I wasn't dead or about to die. More amazing than the angels around me was the feeling I had: I was completely filled up with a feeling of love, and it was so amazing.

The angels were saying to me, 'We love you, we love you so much,' and just repeating it again and again. I opened my eyes to see if they were really there but I was still in the little room. I closed my eyes again because I wanted to go back to the angels, and as soon as I did so they appeared again. They continued speaking to me and saying, 'We're here, we're here, there's no rush, we are here as long as you want us to be.' They were there, and throughout the entire experience I remember thinking I was not afraid of death because I knew that I was seeing and feeling what you see and feel when you die.

I was actually so happy, although the word happy doesn't describe it really. I don't think there is a word for it, but 'blissful' is as close as you would get.

My biggest earthly worry is of losing the people I love, but even that didn't matter in that moment. The whole thing seemed to last about half an hour but I don't know for sure. I guess the therapist must have come back and I was back in reality. I told my husband Keith about it and he said the 'Oh, how nice dear' kind of thing! I think he thought, 'Oh, what a nice dream she had,' but I knew it was more than a dream.

Time went on, and it stayed a pleasant memory. I hadn't told anyone else about it until I spoke to my work colleague Penelope. I looked at her and said, in a very open-hearted, emotional state, 'But how do I know if it was imagined or real?'

Before I had finished speaking she said to me, 'There's your sign, Lorraine.' I looked to where she was pointing, to the left of my head, and there was something floating down to the floor. She said 'It's a white feather.' I bent down to pick it up and thought, 'Oh dear, it's just a bit of cotton, how can I tell her?' But she repeated, 'It's a white feather, Lorraine!' She was sitting 12 or more feet away from me but she knew, and as I looked at it properly I saw it *was* a small white feather. Unbelievable!

No windows were open, no doors had closed; there were no fabrics in the room that the feather could have come from. It didn't float past me; it came straight down as if from the ceiling. I asked Penelope the next day, 'When did you first see the feather?' and she said, 'Just as it passed your head' (on my left). I couldn't stop talking and thinking about it for ages. Even now, I probably think about it every day.

This experience has proved to me, beyond any doubt, that what I experienced that day was real. I now feel so comforted, knowing for sure that my beloved father is there, in the special place we go to, and that we will all go there when it's our time.

Every word I have said here is true, Jacky. I have sticky-taped the feather to a piece of black card and carry it in my handbag so it's with me everywhere I go.

Lorraine, Dubai

If you find a white feather after asking for a sign, maybe you could keep it in a special place, too? Lorraine's idea of taping it to a piece of card is a good one. You could also collect several together in a little muslin bag, or just pop one in your purse. Sometimes I carry them around so that I can give them away to people whose need is greater than mine.

What happens when you're ill or have an accident and it's not your time to die? Do you get chucked out of heaven or do you have to stay? Let's find out ...

Not Your Time

There are only two ways to live your life. One is as though nothing is a miracle. The other is as though everything is a miracle.
— Albert Einstein

I love to read all about your inspirational experiences. Do you have a guardian angel, too? Of course! No one is exempt. Before we are born our souls choose a specific type of life. The life we pick is one which will help us to learn the lessons we need to incorporate into our spiritual selves. Which lessons have you picked for this lifetime? Here are a few:

- forgiveness
- patience
- unconditional love
- charity
- how to love
- innocence
- creativity

- **spirituality**
- **the importance of family**
- **coping with ill-health**
- **disparity.**

Most us will have picked two or three different things to work on so the life we choose and the people we interact with during each lifetime will help us. That friend of yours who annoys you may have offered to interact with you in an annoying way to help bring you the lesson of patience, for example. Isn't that great of him?! Ha, ha – you might start to think of the people you find annoying a little differently now, mightn't you?

One of your lessons might be to learn to live with shortness of breath (you may have asked for a life where you would live at a slower pace to help you learn to appreciate those around you more, for example). Or perhaps you asked for a hearing disorder so that you might concentrate on 'seeing things' more clearly without distraction ... well, you get the idea!

Many of our challenges are 'chosen' by us in advance of life (on a soul level, of course!) or we pick our bodies in advance knowing they will provide us with the type of conditions we need to learn certain life-skills. I admit it's a challenge even believing this, and I know a lot of people who don't like what they see in the mirror will say, 'Seriously ... you want me to believe I picked this body on purpose?!' Well, sort of – you picked the body for living the life which most represented the lessons you wanted to learn. Remember, too, that however you may feel about it sometimes, your body is a gift. Take care of it. As my dear mum reminds me, there are always people worse off than us and we could all do with being grateful for the gifts we've been given.

So our most important lesson might just be to ask ourselves, 'Why might I have chosen this experience in my life right now? What do I need to learn from this?' Some of the most amazing people I know have the biggest physical challenges or ailments. They are often (but not always) some of the more advanced spiritual beings among us!

Yet the angels realize that our bodies can be a trial, and they help whenever they can. I have suffered the trauma associated with constant and continuous pain; this is one of the biggest challenges of all. It's not easy to keep a smile on your face when you can't get out of bed. I have several members of my family going through this trauma at this time and I feel for them. Pain makes every day a sad day. No doubt you will know people who are going through this, too.

PAST LIVES AND HYPNOTHERAPY

Angels seem to be able to help with most things and it's possible to hear of miracle-type healings that occur. Sometimes our illnesses can be related to past lives … yes, journeys our souls have made to other realms and in other time-lines (maybe even on Earth). Lots of people remember past lives spontaneously (particularly very young children). Hypnosis can also be helpful with this. If you have always limped with your right foot in this lifetime but discovered that in a past life (perhaps during a war) you were shot in the leg, this might explain a few things. It sounds unbelievable but many have found relief and healing in this way. Look for trained hypnotherapists who offer this type of 'regression treatment' if you feel it might help you.

Your angels may show you glimpses of past lives in dreams (nothing like ordinary dreams) or during meditation. Meditation is a brilliant way of reaching other realms! Why not give it a go? If you are ill and feeling trapped at home at the moment, why not read up on meditation to see if it will free your mind to go travelling without your body? The internet is a great place to start your research.

LIFE BETWEEN LIVES AND HYPNOTHERAPY

There is a new type of treatment you may not have heard about: Life between Lives, or LBL. This is the place we go between this life and the next, and it's being investigated in several ways. There are many practitioners who use LBL therapy. The hypnotherapist will take the client into the very deepest levels of trance (hypnosis). Most traditional hypnotherapists won't take you to these deeper levels of trance because it's where the 'strange and weird' stuff happens! Of course they have to go this deep because your conscious mind ... the bit that goes 'Am I making this stuff up?' is not aware at these deeper levels, so it's perfect for getting to the truth! This is the scary bit for the untrained therapist, but with an expert it's a fascinating part of the mind to explore.

The therapist will usually 'regress' you (take you back) to an earlier time in your life, then back again and again until you find yourself in the womb. People are amazed that they recall anything of this time, but they do. Everything that you have ever done, said or thought is recorded in some way and, amazingly, can be accessed. The hypnotherapist may then take you to a past life and then explore that life with you, right up until the point when you died. Surprisingly this is not the scary experience you might think it would be. Dying under hypnosis is usually a positive experience.

Once you are 'dead' your soul is often escorted to the heavenly realms by an angel or guide (or deceased relatives). It's common to see before you the life you've just led. There are lots of people living today who've had a 'near-death' experience (i.e. they nearly died or 'died' and were then revived). Many recall being able to see their whole life pass before their lives. During these near-death experiences, your soul gets to witness what's happened in your life (so far) and recall all the thoughts, feelings and actions you've experienced … including those actions which may have hurt, or comforted, others along the way. You actually get to find out how you helped people … or hindered them. Those simple words of praise you said one day to a stranger may turn out to have been one of the most important things you ever did in your life … of great spiritual importance! The deep hypnotic trance state can mimic the experience people go through when they have a near-death experience: seeing your whole life flash before your eyes.

Many who go through this experience (either during a real near-death experience or sometimes during hypnosis) say that they recall things they thought were important that turn out to be not important at all. Loving and caring for others in a physical way (rather than simply sending money to a local charity), putting yourself out, making an effort to help others, these all turn out to be the most important things.

Your therapist can ask you (while under hypnosis), 'Why did you pick this life? What did you hope to learn?' and so on. Authors Dr Michael Newton and Dolores Cannon teach students how to perform these techniques. If you've been through or are suffering from an illness or accident, this might be of interest (especially if you are struggling to get past the 'Why me?' stage of a negative life experience).

WHAT HAPPENS WHEN IT'S NOT YOUR TIME

Of course, a 'near-death' experience occurs when it's *not* actually your 'time' to pass over. Angels are good at helping out in these situations, and I often receive stories of people who witness their angels during this time of bodily trauma. If you are near to death, then it's one of those rare occasions when you *might* see your angels – so don't get confused into thinking that just because you *see* your angel it means you are going to die. *It doesn't* … and you aren't necessarily going to be dying any time soon! Your angel may have appeared to let you know they are helping you to live, or that they are healing you in some way. Their appearance might be just to comfort you. Your angel might appear at this time because your state of mind (that is, unconsciousness) may enable them to reach you, possibly for the first time ever.

Why do some people live and others die? Is it 'our time' or simply a freak of nature, an anomaly? Can angels really save our lives? Here's Kirsty's encounter.

An Angel Saved My Life

I was taken into hospital with septicaemia after having a dream/vision of loved ones who had passed away. My loved ones explained that I had to go to hospital and that there was something seriously wrong with me.

I was 23 when I fell pregnant with my son. I knew from the start that I would have a boy. I dreamed about a tiny baby boy before I discovered I was even expecting. It was a very worrying time for me because I had always been told that I would never have children, due to health problems. I went ahead with the pregnancy despite being advised by medical professionals to have a termination. I did not become ill during those nine months; instead, I flourished and physically felt great. I was worried about the birth, of course.

The day came when I went into labour and I was taken into hospital. The birth was fine, I had a normal delivery but I did have problems with the afterbirth. It would not come away from the womb. The midwife told me that I would have to go to theatre and have it removed. Instead what happened was the doctor came in and said that there was no need for that. It was my first child and you always assume that doctors know best. I didn't go to theatre; it was removed in pieces although the doctor didn't know if he had removed it all. The birth was soon forgotten and I took my baby home. As far as I was concerned he was my little miracle, a gift from the angels.

I hadn't felt right since the birth but just assumed that this was normal. It wasn't something I could really explain; I just didn't feel right within myself.

My son was only three weeks old when I became ill with what I thought was the flu. I woke up that morning feeling terrible. I was stiff and sore all over; I had a sore head and was very sick. I did the obvious thing and called my mother, who looked after my baby and sent me to bed to rest. I found it impossible to rest; I kept worrying about the baby even though I knew my mother was perfectly capable. Within an hour I was feeling so bad that I didn't argue, however; I just went to my bed.

Then the strangest thing happened: I don't know if I was dreaming or awake; I don't remember falling asleep and know that I had only been in bed for about 20 minutes because I kept checking the clock. I was just aware of faces appearing directly in front of me, and I felt very calm. They told me that I had to go to hospital, warning me that it was important that I went very soon because something was wrong. The whole thing was very vivid and did not feel like a dream. If I did fall asleep I don't remember waking, either.

The dream/vision, or whatever it was, was so real that I was completely convinced that I had to go to hospital. My mother thought I was worrying about nothing; it was winter and there was a lot of flu going around. She had to go to work so a friend took the baby to her own house and, as my mother was on her way out, I begged her to please just call a doctor. I knew that she wouldn't be back for hours and I would be on my own. She agreed to call the doctor even though she didn't think there was any need. She didn't make her work that day. By the time the doctor arrived at the house I was being violently sick and was in a lot of pain. He called an ambulance and had me taken straight into the Accident and Emergency department.

It was discovered that I had septicaemia and I remained in hospital for quite a while. I kept seeing white feathers on the floor of my hospital room – where could they have come from? There were no feathers in the pillows or anything like that; they just seemed to appear from nowhere. As I had other health problems, which complicated the whole thing, I was transferred to the ward of a doctor whom I knew very well.

When I was eventually on the mend I had a good chat with him, and he told me that if the doctors had reached me any later I would have died. I was totally shocked, especially when they told me the doctors hadn't expected me to pull through. Due to complications I had to have two major operations to save my legs, which I almost lost. It took me well over a year to get back on my feet properly; I had to learn to walk all over again.

If it wasn't for my warning from the angels I wouldn't be here today. If I'd allowed my mother to leave for work that day I would never have made it to hospital in time. It was that warning that convinced me to go to hospital. My son is ten years old now, and I will never forget how the angels helped me through my pregnancy and then saved my life. My beautiful baby was not the only miracle in my life, and my faith will always be strong after what we came through. There will never be any doubt in my mind about the existence of angels.

Kirsty, Scotland

I was really moved reading Kirsty's story. Imagine if that little baby had been left without his mother? It's a fine line between calling for help and not 'bothering' the doctor because we feel our condition is not serious! How easy would it have been to have written this experience off as just a dream? Maybe it's time to pay attention to our 'dreams', especially when we recall them so vividly! (Now that I have said that, please don't panic ... mainly dreams are just a mixture of our worries, fears and experiences, all mixed up together). If ever you're not sure or the 'dream' is a message about your health, go and get it checked out just in case.

Here's another story where it's *not* someone's time ... and they are actually told that while unconscious. I've picked the title for the story from the phrase the angels repeat over and over again. If they tell you it's not your time, then believe them.

Not Your Time

When I was 21 I was a bit of a tearaway and I had my own motorbike, which my mother hated. She used to say, 'Jeanie I don't like you going on that bike, one day you will get hurt,' but I just ignored her every time.

This particular night started off normally enough. It was a typical May evening, warm and dry, and I decided to go to see my boyfriend by riding over on my bike as I had done many times before. Unfortunately, on this particular night I ended up having a very bad accident. I broke a lot of bones in my body and had serious internal injuries, too.

While I was in the operating theatre I had a strange experience: I found myself being lifted out of my body by the most wonderful white, glowing but soft angel. She had no wings, just a bright glimmering white light around her. I could make out her face and hair and her arms, and when she turned me around I could see myself in the operating theatre below. The surgeon was using the paddles on me to try and start my heart ... I'd flat-lined.

The angel showed me my mum and family, and I noticed that my mum still had her slippers on! The angel turned me around and spoke to me; her voice was like a breeze but I could hear her clearly as she said to me, 'This is not your time, Jeanie, you have a gift and you must use it to help and heal others; you have a job to fulfil.' Then she put her arms around me again and that's really all I remember.

When I came out of intensive care I knew that I had died during the operation, so I asked the doctor whether I had and he verified my experience. He said to me, 'You have a strong heart,' and reassured me that I was going to be OK. Later on I spoke to my mum about what had happened to me, and she sat very silently before telling me, 'The mind plays tricks when you've had anaesthetic' – but she believed me when I told her that I had seen the slippers on her feet and what she had been wearing!

Later that night I felt the angel's presence around me. Then I knew that I had to learn more, so I began my journey finding out and learning about angels. I decided to do a course and went to my local spiritual church and studied hard. I had a real thirst for knowledge and wanted to bring the angels into my life.

The next experience I had was when my stepfather was dying of cancer and I knew he was going to be leaving his earthly body soon. In June of 2004 he was taken into a hospice because, sadly, he was now too ill to be taken care of at home. My mother and I decided to go into town to do some shopping before we went to visit him, but I had already said to Mum that we'd better make it quick because I knew we had to get there. I had an urgent feeling inside.

When we got to the hospice the nurse told us he'd already passed over, but as we entered the room I saw him (his spirit body) standing by the bed and looking at his body. It was then that he turned and looked at us as if he were in a haze. He came round to my mum and as my mum was holding his hand he laid his spirit hands on her shoulders and he smiled and then just faded into the light. His physical body was lying on the bed and he had a peaceful smile and I said to my mum, 'He hung on for us, mum, he didn't pass over until we had arrived because he wanted to say goodbye.'

I still have contact with the angel that saved me. Her name is Salina and I have been guided by her ever since. I've passed many angel courses and now have my own website which is just dedicated to the angels. I believe I am guided by them all the time.

Jeanie, England

I love that, like me, Jeanie's experiences changed her life to the extent that she is now helping other people who've had angel encounters.

People can have the most bizarre experiences when they are unconscious … it always seems like the mind might just be playing tricks … or is it? It makes you question the experience more, though, when you discover others have had similar types of 'dreams' and encounters when they are unconscious. The fun part is when you come back with some sort of proof – like Jeanie's vision of her mother's slippers.

You are not alone. Are these visits to a heavenly realm or an in-between realm? I think so. The more of these experiences I read about, the more similarities I discover! I love reading about the hidden realms – it's much more fun than watching TV shows where they mooch around people's homes! Imagine getting glimpses of other realms and dimensions. If only people could take their cameras!

Steve shares his experience here – though it's not all good …

Strange Realm

Two years ago I had a heart attack and was declared dead for over 30 minutes. Yet the paramedics still managed to resuscitate me. Amazing! After being brought back to life I was in a coma for three days, and during that time I had the most bizarre experience …

At first I was walking along a road or route, and on each side of this road there were grotesque-looking people. From what they were wearing they seemed to represent different times in history, mainly in my view early nineteenth-century clothing, or rags really. These people appeared to be in a state of pain or horror and were wandering around, but they couldn't touch me. The whole place was like the photos you see of the lunar landscape, it was coloured black and red and in the distance you could see a light shining on what seemed to be the horizon.

One character in particular came quite close to me; he was wearing clothes which I can only describe as like those worn by actors in the *Oliver Twist* films. The character who played Bill Sikes [the strong and aggressive fictional character in the novel by Charles Dickens], I know this is a fictional character but the clothes and face were quite similar. I was aware of something standing behind me but I didn't turn round.

The next thing I recall was being back in my body and conscious in hospital. I don't know if this was a dream or a real experience, but when I investigated what happened to me on the internet it seemed that the medium Edgar Cayce had a similar experience and described what I saw, so I don't know!

Steve, France

Fascinating isn't it? Edgar Cayce was a famous American seer who channelled hundreds of messages to living visitors who came to see him; he also answered questions about illnesses and other things, including suggesting cures (some of which included ingredients which Cayce could never have known about).

Steve and Edgar Cayce are not the only ones. Various people previously have encountered breathtaking heavenly gardens, buildings which reminded them of images of ancient Rome, gorgeous colours they have never witnessed on Earth and buildings made of crystal! Have you visited heaven or been shown a glimpse of the other side by your loved ones? Write and let me know!

BABY'S ANGELS

Even unborn babies have guardian angels, and they're not against performing the odd miracle or two. This next story is fascinating … who helped this little one from inside the womb?

Miracle Baby

I am the very proud auntie of three little boys: Spencer (aged four), Jackson (three) and Cameron (one). This experience is about what happened to my sister during her pregnancy with her youngest son, Cameron.

When we found out that Tanya was pregnant, we were overjoyed. She already had two little boys and seemed to be ready for another. She had had fairly easy pregnancies with Spencer and Jackson, and this pregnancy was also going quite smoothly. When Tanya went for her six-month ultrasound, she was given some news that was absolutely heartbreaking. A specialist was called in to review the ultrasound, and said that it revealed a cyst on Cameron's brain. Some more intensive ultrasounds were done and they revealed that there were some arteries in his brain that were too small to function, and also that his arms (forearms in particular), were slightly shorter than average. The general conclusion that was given to Tanya and her husband, Cory, was that Cameron was likely to have developmental delays, and possibly Down's syndrome.

I can't even begin to explain the sort of shock that went over my entire body when I heard the news. It was so surreal, and absolutely devastating. My sister couldn't help but think that it was something that she had done wrong during the pregnancy that may have caused the issues, but of course she'd done nothing.

Our entire family and all of her doctors and specialists reassured her that it was in no way her fault. We made sure to drive the point across that everything happens for a reason and that if God's plan was for Cameron to be this way, then that's the way it was going to be. There was no room for extra stress, and no room for guilt. My sister was told that she might not be able to carry Cameron to full term, and that there was even a possibility that she would lose the baby. We were all heartbroken.

At the eight-and-a-half month checkpoint, ultrasounds detected that the cyst had almost completely disappeared, the blood flow around his brain appeared to be normal, and it didn't look as if Tanya was going to be delivering until her due date. We were shocked. How did this turnaround happen? What intervention had brought about this amazing conclusion? ... but still, he wasn't born yet.

The part that absolutely amazes me begins on the day that Cameron was born: 14th August 2009. The significance of this date is absolutely incredible. My grandmother, Patricia Faye Wallis, struggled with many health problems in her short life. She fought hard and, despite being in a coma after a massive stroke in July 2000, she managed to mumble out her last words: 'Hi Les' to my mom, her former daughter-in-law, before she died. We all knew that she wasn't going to be able to hang on for very much longer, and that became a reality on 14th August 2000.

My grandmother was an angel. I never once heard her complain about being in pain. She was joking and laughing with me two days after open-heart surgery! My entire family misses her dearly, and thinks about her daily. (Often we can smell the perfume she wore ... in the most random of places, too!) Anyway, her connection to Cameron, in a more logical sense, is that he was born nine years to the day that she died.

Here's where the miraculous part comes in: Cameron was born with ABSOLUTELY NO signs of brain defects, and he just happened to be the largest out of all three boys! His arms were a little on the short side, but that hasn't proved to be any type of burden on his mobility ... and especially not on his food intake! That in itself is a miracle that our family likes to thank Grandma for regularly ... we feel sure that she was the one to intervene.

Another twist to the story is that, when Cameron was going for his six-month check-up, my sister decided to ask our doctor about a little spot above her lip that hadn't gone away since Cameron had been born. She was referred to a dermatologist, and a biopsy was taken from her lip and from a spot on her forehead. The results came back a few days later and it turns out that the spots were basal cell carcinomas (a type of treatable skin cancer). If Cameron had not been born, or even if Tanya had not gotten pregnant with him to start with, the spot above her lip would never have been checked.

If all of these occurrences are just coincidence ... then thank God for coincidences. But I believe that it was the work of Grandma, Tanya's angel, who protected baby Cam and my sister. Miracles do happen ... I can't even imagine my life without my angels.

Jillian, Canada

I'm not a doctor but this healing-in-the-womb story sounds pretty miraculous to me, angel or not!

ANGELS IN DISGUISE

Have you ever seen an angel in disguise? Of course you might ask me, Jacky, how would we know if it's in disguise? Exactly ... pretty good question! Angels can appear in many different ways, so if you want to see an angel you may need to stay alert! Perhaps you have already seen one and have no idea?

This woman believes she was protected by an angel during a dangerous point in her life. Was this an angel in disguise? How did the young girl know what to do at a time of danger ... was her angel warning her?

Saved by a Multi-coloured Angel?

When I was nine years old I walked the short distance home from school to find that my mother was not yet home from work. As it was a nice summer's day I decided to go and wait for her at the bus stop where she always got off. As I was waiting I noticed that in the distance a man was walking in my direction and that he kept looking behind him and looking around. As he got closer I started to feel slightly uneasy, and noticed that the only other person in sight was a blind man on the opposite side of the road.

Just then the most beautiful little bird landed about a metre in front of me and just stood looking at me. It was a bird of many colours and one which I haven't seen since. I was fixated on the bird momentarily and then it flew off. As it flew off I got an overwhelming instinctive feeling that I needed to run, and so I did. I wasn't really too sure why I was running at the time but I just did what I felt. As I looked behind me the man, who had been walking towards me previously, was also running. My little legs were now shaking with fear but I just kept on running until a passerby saw what was happening and ran to my aid. The man behind me immediately ran off towards the local beach.

When we later informed the police we were told that a convicted paedophile matched the description I had given. He had recently been released in the area and he'd already attempted to coax a young girl into a car in the same area just two nights previous to my experience. I've reflected on the incident over the years since and I truly believe that the unusual rainbow-coloured bird was an angel in disguise.

Paula, England

I'm sure that Paula is right here. A young girl is unlikely to feel the instinct to run and at that age would more likely feel compelled to stay and be polite to the man (as we are taught in childhood: Be polite to adults!). Thank goodness Paula got away safely. What a magical and safe way to see an angel.

ANIMAL ANGELS

Just a fun little distraction here: I get numerous stories about angel animals ... or of people's lives being saved by animals in a mysterious way, so I can't resist sneaking in a few more here.

You may have seen this next one in the news. Actor Dick Van Dyke, legendary star of *Chitty Chitty Bang Bang* and *Mary Poppins*, was talking to talk show host Craig Ferguson about his experiences with a long board out in the ocean. Dick said on the show that one day he was out in the ocean and fell asleep on the board. When he woke up he was well out to sea, which immediately is a frightening prospect. He very quickly became aware that he was not alone out in the water, either, and noticed that he was surrounded by fins. Dick said he was terrified at first that he might die, I guess either from drowning or from the creatures with the fins – either thought being terrifying!

But all was not as it seemed at first. 'They turned out to be porpoises,' he explained. 'And they pushed me all the way to shore.' He turned to assure the shocked audience that he was serious, it really did happen! He was protected by some very special animal-angels that day out at sea.

National Geographic have produced a DVD about animals around the world who have saved the lives of humans. Most notable of these was the case of five-year-old Levan Merritt, who toppled head-first into a gorilla cage at Jersey Zoo in 1986. You may have heard of this. Levan's family thought the young boy was dead, yet he was protected by the large silverback Jambo, who kept the other gorillas away until medics could safely remove the boy. The whole incident was filmed by a passerby (you can search for this on YouTube). Jambo is shown reaching over and stroking the boy tenderly. It's magical to watch.

Incidentally, if you ever need cheering up take a browse through YouTube (online film clips) and see some of the angel-magic of the animal kingdom. Meet the painting elephants from Thailand – yes, really! Keepers set up easels and keep pots of paint and brushes handy. After loading the brush with paint the elephant's human 'assistant' hands the brush over to the art-loving elephant. As you would expect, abstract images are not a problem, but amazingly the elephants will also paint lifelike images of each other. Yes, the elephants paint pictures of other elephants as well as landscapes and even readable human words (taught by the keepers). I saw a clip of one elephant painting the words HAPPY NEW YEAR!

My favourite is a painting of three elephants painted from behind, mother in the middle and two babies, one each side ... their three tails all in a row. I want that painting! These elephants live at the Thai Elephant Conservation Centre. Anyway, I get beautifully distracted ... as I always do with animal stories!

Here is another life-saving story ... the last animal-related one for this book: Judy is a collie/greyhound cross who saved her mistress' life. Carol Smith had a stroke and fell out of bed. Lying on the floor in the cold and dark, Carol was in great danger and only the family pet Judy was awake to notice. Rushing round to the side of the bed where Carol's husband lay sleeping the dog placed her paw on his face, banging down repeatedly until he awoke. Then Judy kept running to the other side of the bed. When Mr Smith looked over he noticed his wife was missing but thought at first she was in the bathroom. Luckily the dog (a rescue) was persistent and Carol's husband found his wife on the floor. Carol was rushed to hospital ... no doubt just in time! What an angel Judy was!

ANGEL STRANGERS

If you saw an angel, you'd know, wouldn't you? Don't angels have wings and halos and a certain glow about them? Not necessarily ... read on.

Mysterious Strangers

Of course you don't die. Nobody dies. Death doesn't exist.
You only reach a new level of vision, a new realm of
consciousness, a new unknown world.
— Henry Miller

You've read the books, you may even have worn the t-shirt. Protected by angels, you believe. Yet where are the angels? Why can't we see them?

THE VISIBLE LIGHT SPECTRUM

This week (February 2011) I appeared on ITV's *This Morning* daytime magazine programme, with celebrity guest 'believer' Gloria Hunniford. The two of us were invited onto the show to be interviewed by presenters Phillip Schofield and Holly Willoughby about our experiences and belief in angels. One of the viewers' questions related to why some people can see angels and others can't. It's a great question but the answer is that most of us can't; angels reside outside of the 'visible' light spectrum ... visible to humans, that is.

There is a brilliant image on the Arthur Findlay Society website, part of a short feature called *Where Is the Etheric World?* The extract on the website is taken from Findlay's book *The Rock of Truth* ... and it describes where the angels are – sort of, anyway.

First of all, let me explain who Arthur Findlay was, for those of you who do not know. Arthur Findlay, OBE, lived 16th May 1883 to 24th July 1964. Way back in the 1920s, scientists discovered that what we know as solid matter is not solid at all. It consists of atoms which are broken down further into particles or waves. (Your table-top looks solid enough to the naked eye, but like all 'solid' objects, it's actually moving and full of holes ... as a strong enough microscope would reveal, anyway!)

Findlay believed that the etheric world (or spirit world) exists in the same way that radio waves do: that it interpenetrates our world but is beyond our human perception (humankind's limited ability to perceive). I write a little bit about this subject in all of my books; it's confusing but eventually we'll all understand it OK, right?

Findlay's 'informants' on the other side explained it to him. The chart (on the Findlay Society website) explains this further. A line running top to bottom of the page represents the light spectrum as we know it so far. It is split up into divisions, the middle section of which is the bit we can see (the colours of the rainbow). The band of light which is visible to humans is very small (visible light, split into colours between 34,000 and 64,000 waves to the inch, or from 400 to 750 billion waves to the second ... bear with me, here, as I know you're starting to switch off!).

Not all humans can see every colour in what we call the 'normal' human range. Some people are 'colour-blind', which means they see an even narrower band of light (their eyes mix up certain colours, pink and green for example). Colours are just different wavelengths of light.

Either side of this narrow central visible band of light, Findlay added the bands (range) called ultraviolet and infrared (which of course we can measure scientifically and know exist ... they are 'real'). Either side of that (with faster and slower vibrations than we can perceive) are heat waves, short radio waves, microwaves and long radio waves. And, beyond the ultraviolet range, the etheric world, x-rays and gamma waves. It kind of makes sense doesn't it? No? OK, try not to fall asleep at this bit.

Because this etheric range (it is believed) sits next to the narrow band most humans can see, there will be some humans who *can* see a little more than the average. Just as some people are colour-blind (with limited colour range, as mentioned), it seems only sensible that some people will be 'colour-enlightened' (my made-up word!) with the ability to see a slightly larger range of the light spectrum. In just this way we have clairvoyants: those with the ability to see or dip into the etheric range from time to time. Phew! Nearly there!

Colour-blindness is actually quite complicated, not least in that it varies from person to person. The most common type makes it difficult to distinguish between red and green; the cones (colour receptors) in the eyes of people with this variation are not sensitive to long wavelengths (red). Problems with seeing green mean the cones are insensitive to medium wavelengths, and those whose eyes struggle to pick up blues are insensitive to short wavelengths. There is also a very small group of people who can see no colours at all. Got it? No?

OK, scientifically speaking (sort of), the angels' vibration/realms lie next to ours, which is why sometimes people can see them! Findlay believed that life was continuous ... and I know he is right. I believe that our angels, guides and deceased loved ones sit in this etheric band ... at ever-increasing vibrations. The more advanced the soul, the higher in this band it resides (though 'reside' is not a good word, dear reader, as I don't mean to imply they live in houses; perhaps 'exist' would be better).

OK, that's enough for now! I don't want to 'blind' you with science ...

By the way, at the end of each week the presenters on *This Morning* are asked to talk about their favourite bits of the show from each day (the clips are added to their website), and Holly Willoughby said that the angels segment had been her favourite. She even explained how she'd found a white angel feather on her dress earlier in the day before the show started ... a strange coincidence, I thought!

CAN YOU SEE ANGELS?

Your physical human body is what decides if you can see angels or not ... the ability of your human eyes, as discussed. You can't just *decide* you want to see them and suddenly be able to do so. Yet you can increase your chances of physically seeing beings from these realms ... just a little bit. Meditation helps a lot – the more you meditate the 'further up' you can visit these higher vibrational realms. Changes in consciousness (being in a coma or unconscious, during trauma and occasionally during illness and sometimes when you are on the verge of sleep or awakening) can, briefly, make visible the angelic realm or the angels themselves. Most of my own communications happen when I am asleep (in another state of altered consciousness).

Can you see angels, then? Some people see rainbow-coloured lights, twinkling stars or glittering energy when angels appear. Maybe you are lucky enough to sense them in this way? Others, it's true, will see a full manifestation of a being of light ... now that's lucky (or is it just 'good eyes' – who knows?).

CAN YOU SENSE ANGELS?
So you might not be able to see angels but you might be able to sense them. If an angelic being enters the space around your aura (the human energy field), you may pick up an impression of their being. We sense all sorts of things all the time. You can invite angels into your life (rather than summon them) and this can help.

Human beings appear to have limited 'electroreception' (or 'electroception'), although many scientists will disagree with me there! Electroreception is the ability to sense electric fields. Some people seem to be able to pick up the human energy field. When someone else is close by we can often sense them (pick up their energy field) before we see them – you know that someone is behind you or you know someone is watching you because you sense it rather than see it.

We already know that several species of fish, along with sharks and rays, can pick up changes in the electrical fields around them. Some types of fish even create their own electric fields. We don't know enough about the senses of the human body, and over the next few years I'm hoping to be able to expand on this area more.

CAN YOU SMELL THEM?
Strange as it might seem, yes, you can smell angels. Sometimes angels bring along the gift of scent. The smell of beautiful flowers

is the most common. Be aware ... not everyone can smell this scent (as with the vision perception, above). The scent may be strong to you alone or to just a couple of you, while everyone else thinks you're crazy as they can smell nothing!

CAN YOU HEAR THEM?

Sound is, of course, just another vibration. Tinkling bells and angelic choir sounds can often be heard when an angel (or angels) are around, especially when angels draw close to collect the deceased or when they are working on healing. Occasionally, especially during emergencies, people will hear the odd word or two. Speaking is not a natural phenomenon for angels; they communicate using a type of telepathy, so any words they do use will be brief: *Don't worry, everything will be OK, We are here for you, All will be well, You will live* ... and, most classically, *It's not your time.*

We imagine that we can hear only through our physical ears, but sound (especially in the lower frequencies) can also be picked up as vibrations carried through the body by tactition (the sense of pressure perception) or, in other words, you can *feel* the sound. Try sitting in a room with cotton wool or earplugs in and turn up the volume of something with a powerful drum beat ... you'll feel the sound, trust me.

MORE ON MYSTERIOUS STRANGERS

Encountering an angel is a life-changing experience. Living with the phenomenon is another thing entirely. Now, I realize there will be some of you reading this book who will be wondering, Jacky, have you entirely lost the plot? No! (Although my husband might disagree.) Millions, yes millions, of people have experienced miracle-type occurrences and angel visitations in their lives ... even if each person has only one magical encounter. Seriously, if you kept a record of the magic in your own life you might well be very surprised at how often paranormal phenomena (experiences unexplainable by current science) happen in your life, too.

Humans are easily unhinged ... now, I'm not being rude, but it doesn't take much for us to 'lose it'. Anything too strange happens and we just switch off, we deny it, we can't believe it's real ... so we don't try. The same thing happens when we hear bad news. What is the natural response? 'No ... I don't believe it ...' Or, as they say in the sci-fi movies, our brains can't 'compute' the information. It just doesn't fit our idea of what our world should be. Some people literally flip the daylight switch (ever seen someone faint with shock?).

Is it any wonder, then, that angel visits are subtle? Is it not easier to believe that the whole thing might have been a dream? It's certainly easier for our fragile brains to accept, anyway.

Occasionally angels appear as mysterious strangers in human form. Of course we can better accept angels in this human-type state rather than the more alien appearance that angels might really own. Not all angels look like the statues we create, but many people do feel a kind of safety in the presence of the classic glowing human-shaped figures with large white wings!

Your angel might appear as a street walker or a religious figure. He or she might momentarily pop in as a child or even an animal. Would you recognize your angel if he or she appeared like this? Maybe not at first, anyway. It might only be afterwards that you consider the possibility. Was that an angel who saved me on the road? Did a real-life person or an angel lift me out of danger or save me from that car crash, or help me with directions or guide me safely home ...? I could go on and on.

This story was posted on Facebook by Martin. I have his permission to reprint it here (with a little light editing).

Hitchhiker

I would like to share with you all a true story. When I was 16 (I'm 45 now) a mate, Fergus, asked me if I would like to join him backpacking across France for two weeks. I'd just left school, I hadn't started my first job, so with the limited funds I had from my Saturday job, I agreed. I won't take you through the whole two weeks, but needless to say it was a rollercoaster ride: just two carefree 16-year-old lads and it was mostly fun.

Now let me jump forward. We were on the last Friday of our trip, having already made it to St Tropez (mostly with the power of our thumbs). We had to get back to the UK for the Monday and we weren't having any luck hitchhiking together that morning. Rather naively we agreed to split up and meet up again in Paris, at one of the central train stations.

My friend headed for the autoroute and left me on an A-road. This was in the day when we had no mobile phones, no cash-point machines and no internet cafés to access computers ... in fact we had no e-mail. As you can imagine, I was scared. To say this was my Everest would be an understatement, but I pressed on. Rather than saying to myself, 'There is no way we will meet in Paris,' I just kept asking for what I really wanted and needed to happen, which was a lift to Paris. I had the idea firmly fixed in my head and wouldn't allow myself to think of what might go wrong. Paris was about a day's drive away, hundreds of miles.

I continued to wait and around 40 minutes later a guy pulled up in a little car and asked if I wanted a lift. I gratefully accepted his help, and he asked me where I was heading. When I told him Paris, he simply said, 'No problem, so am I.' No problem? Not only did he treat me to lunch but he dropped me at the station at the end of a very long journey. This stranger expected or asked for nothing in return.

I spent the night in the bus shelter, as my friend arrived a day later. He had been jumping trains to get to Paris and couldn't believe my story. To this day I am in awe of the power of thought!

Martin was kind enough to allow me to print his story, and then followed it up with a PS:

... I'm in a reflecting, dare I say nostalgic mood: on that same trip, one day my friend Fergus and I were dropped at a toll area by the entrance to the autoroute. It was late, we pitched our tent behind some bushes not far from the public washrooms. During the night I was awoken by a noise. It was a large group of bikers who were going crazy in the car park next to our tent. I honestly thought we were going to die, but something inside of me told me we would be OK and believed it would be all right. The noise of the revving bikes and shouting seemed to go on forever, and the following morning we found blood in the car park and in the washrooms! For some unexplained reason we were left alone! I think my angel was enjoying being in France with me!

Martin, England (France!)

If angels were helping with these scenarios, maybe they preferred to remain unseen ... or did they? Who was the kindly driver who paid for lunch? Maybe just a dad with a son of the same age who took pity on the young boy ... or maybe not!

OK, so now here is another of those mysterious voice stories. This one takes place in Australia.

Officer Fire-Angel

I'd like to tell you what happened to me. Some time in 1986 my husband and I took our three children, Michael who was eight and my twins Mark and Kristy who were two years old, on a vacation in our old camper van. The van was decked out with an old auxiliary battery in the back, which we used to run our television and fridge. At night we all slept in a large tent.

On this particular afternoon we all went to have a shower. The shower block was at the top of the caravan park so we used to drive there. After showering I was really looking forward to a nice cup of tea. After such a busy day, the twins fell asleep in the back of the camper van. It seemed a shame to disturb them so I thought I would leave them while I got their beds ready ... and made my cup of tea!

While my husband and I and our son Michael were drinking I heard a voice in my head speak urgently. It said, 'Linda, the kids!' I jumped up and went straight over to the van to check and, to my horror, the auxiliary battery must have overheated, as it was on fire. I yelled to Steven and we quickly managed to get the kids to safety. Then afterwards we pulled the faulty battery out of the van.

It was really only later that I thought about that voice in my head and realized that the voice saved my twins' lives.

The voice did sound familiar to me, but I couldn't recall why. Whoever it was, I will always be grateful.

Linda, Australia

Was this another angel or something else? Let's have a look at a few more stories, each with its own unique twist! Are there telephones in heaven? Let's see.

Wrong Number?

I was very close to my mum and used to rely on her guidance and comfort. I suffer from a couple of chronic pain conditions and when she was alive I used to ring her up when I was in pain or upset. She would give me a 'phone-hug' if I needed that.

One day, long after my mother had passed away, when my husband was at work, I literally got stuck on the loo (my arthritic hip locked!) and I sat there bawling my eyes out and said out loud, 'Mum, I wish you were here.'

Later that night my husband and I were woken by the phone ringing. It was 2 in the morning. I got out of bed and made my way to the phone. A man asked for 'Brenda', which isn't my name. I should have been irritated at being woken up, but I wasn't. Walking back to bed, I realized that our answer-phone hadn't clicked on after three rings. Normally my husband goes to answer the phone because he is faster than me; I knew that the angels had fixed the wrong number to give comfort to me. The man had asked for Brenda and, guess what? My mum's name was, yes it was, Brenda. I went back to bed and fell into a peaceful sleep, knowing that my mum is still around.

Amanda, England

Phones feature in a lot of stories now. Has technology finally caught up on the other side?

Phones in Heaven

My son Regan passed away at 16 years old, two years ago. Anyone who has lost a child will know how you never really get over it. At first there is the awful shock and you just close down, but then later you start to wonder if your loved one is OK. Is he safe? Did he make it to heaven?

Just recently I had the strangest dream. I was fast asleep when I heard my phone ring. Then when I answered it, it was Regan. He spoke to me, saying, 'Hi Mum!'

I was shocked because I'd thought I was asleep but this just felt so real. I said, 'Is this you Reg? Where are you ringing from?'

He replied, 'From heaven, Mum. There are phones in heaven.'

I couldn't believe it. All the questions I had wanted to ask him when he'd died – now was my chance.

'Did you mean to do what you did?' I questioned him.

'NO!' he replied immediately, 'I was trying to stop but it was too late.'

We chatted for a while and then further on through my dream he started speaking through the washing machine! He said, 'I'm here now, Mum!' And it's like he was telling me that he didn't need the phone, he was everywhere. This dream was very real.

Marilyn, New Zealand

Of course it was real! Ordinary dreaming about loved ones is a very different experience compared to this. Marilyn had a dream-visitation – a real visit from her son's spirit when she was asleep. Marilyn was completely lucid and aware throughout, and even thought to ask questions which had been playing on her mind. Our loved ones are everywhere, just as Regan so cleverly explained it. Are there telephones in heaven? Maybe there are. After years of research I now know the difference between a dream and a visitation, but not everyone can tell at first. You're the best person to decide, the person having the experience (or encounter). Say you were in danger and the experience saved your life ... would it matter if the experience was real or a dream? We've already seen that angels can appear as part of a dream anyway. What do you think of this next story?

Carried Away ...

My husband and I were staying overnight in a bed and breakfast a few years ago. One night I woke up and realized that my duvet had been wrapped around my body and I was being carried towards the bedroom door and put down. I also remembered shouting the word 'NO' loudly. My husband woke up and asked me what had happened and I told him but could not explain it, I think I was still in shock so we just went back to bed.

The next morning we found that unknown persons had broken into the apartment and taken the TV set and my mobile phone, amongst other things. It's then that I realized it must have been my guardian angel who had helped to protect us. The feeling of being lifted and carried through the air is what woke me up, and I know that my shouting scared the robbers away. It was just an amazing feeling ... although a little scary! At first I thought I was dreaming but now I realize it was so much more than that!

Salome, South Africa

So many angel experiences happen when people are in bed ... sometimes for rescue purposes like Salome's story. It makes you wonder if sleeping is such a safe thing to do after all, right?

Claire's story was especially worrying.

Smoke Angel

I lived at home with my widowed mother when during the night as I was asleep in my bed I was awoken by what I thought was a sort of mist at the side of my bed. In the middle of this mist I could see what looked like a figure of Our Lady (I am Catholic and this is the only way I could describe this figure at that time). I was startled, but not afraid.

Then I began to realize that the mist was not mist at all, but smoke! This figure was life-sized with large wings, and her hands were outstretched. I got out of bed then and ran into my mother's bedroom, which was also filled with smoke. My mother was fast asleep but I quickly roused her.

When I looked at her bed I immediately realized that the electric blanket was smouldering and on fire. I telephoned the fire service who attended right away so luckily my mother was safe. Fortunately we caught this fire in time.

I have been married for 28 years and this occurrence happened about 30 years ago when I was single and at home.

I have told my children of this night, but I always thought that everyone would laugh at me if I told them that someone woke me and I thought it was Our Lady. That was the vision I saw, but recently I discovered angels and it occurred to me that this could have been my guardian angel ... or my mother's angel, looking out for us that night. I am normally a heavy sleeper and would certainly not have been aware of the smoke.

Claire, Scotland

Have you checked your electric blanket recently? Remember that they have a fairly short lifespan and need to be replaced after a certain length of time. Always switch off the blanket when you go to bed. A friend of mine wasn't so lucky and the fire caused by her electric blanket burned down half her house! Luckily Claire and her mum were safe thanks to the woman in the smoke. OK, time for another story.

Tea in Heaven

One night I dreamed that I was having tea with my mother-in-law, who had recently died. I knew she was dead, and there were people there whom I didn't know. I kept asking them if they were allowed to drink tea after they had died. This is the only part of the conversation that I remember. She came again in a dream with my paternal grandmother, and again I knew they were both dead.

Spirits do all sorts of things they did on Earth when they first passed over, even 'wearing clothes'. These things are comforting to the deceased and are helpful in the initial transition from the human body to the spirit state. Eventually the deceased accept that they are now spirit (a light energy) and no longer need to wear clothes or even eat food.

Here is another letter. Cristina gets the chance to say goodbye to a family member:

Grandmother's Last Goodbye

I've just finished looking at your website and was moved, and it made me feel that maybe I'm not alone after all.

My grandmother passed away when I was 19 years old, and a few days after her death I had a dream that she came to my parents' house, where I was living at the time. In the dream, everything was bright and vivid ... very colourful, almost like bright sunlight was shining in the house, and there was soft beautiful music playing in the background.

The whole experience gave me the sense of total happiness. She was dressed in a yellow business-type suit and had a suitcase. She was smiling. She put the suitcase down and gave me a big hug and told me that she'd just popped in to say goodbye because she had to leave. I remember feeling very warm and happy, and then I woke up.

Notice how vivid the experience was! Over the years I've had quite a few grandparents appearing in dreams to tell their grandchildren that they are passing over, and several who've brought their suitcases! Cristina continued her story to me with another dream-visitation, this time from her grandfather:

A Chat with Grandfather

Several months later my son had gone into hospital and had his tracheotomy removed (he'd had a tracheotomy previously as an aid to his multiple surgeries). It was then that I had another dream; as before it was bright and vivid and full of colour. I can recall the clothes my grandfather was wearing, and that he looked healthy. It was so real; he was sitting on his usual chair wearing clothes I remembered ... but he didn't have his glasses on.

He asked me how my son Gabe was doing, and I told him he was doing well, and that he'd had the 'trach-tube' taken out. That made Grandfather so happy! He just smiled and said how great it was and that he knew that Gabe didn't need it any longer. I remember just a warm, happy feeling, and before he left he gave me a hug and that was it.

Alison wrote to me with this amazing letter; it reminded me of a story in my own family, so I wanted to share it with you here.

Last Dance

I had a dream that I 'married' my husband again (we've been together for 20 years, and we renewed our vows a few years ago). I don't remember the ceremony in my dream but I found myself at the reception afterwards. It was quite traditional, Mum on one side and Dad on the other. I knew Dad was 'visiting' and I was so pleased he was there, but I knew he couldn't stay long.

All of a sudden the DJ put on Frank Sinatra's 'New York, New York' and I jumped to my feet, grabbed my dad's hand and led him to the dance floor. We had the most wonderful dance ever! Funnily enough I never did dance with my dad at my original wedding as he didn't come to the evening party. In my dream I remember thinking, 'I don't care if it's not the right time for the "father/daughter dance", I'm not going to miss this opportunity!'

What a wonderful experience, I feel blessed. I know that Dad has always been around me and always will be.

My own father was a great ballroom dancer and, after he passed on, two of my sisters had dream-visitation experiences where he danced 'ballroom-style' with them. I recall both sisters tell me how amazing it was still to be able to feel his physical touch even though he had died. I hope one day Dad will come to me in a visitation like this so that we can dance, too. (He's visited many times since he passed over, just not to dance.)

Paul, the editor of *Eternal Spirit* magazine, wrote to me with this interesting account, which shows that our relatives really do know when to expect us. Bert was in hospital near the end of his life, so on this occasion it seems his own deceased mother was the method for imparting the information to him that his time was close (otherwise I imagine this sort of information might be a little scary!).

Not Quite Time

I came back from my Uncle Bert's funeral last night, which was in Somerset. Just before he passed he was in hospital drifting in and out of consciousness. He told his stepdaughter that he went to see his mother (deceased) but was told that she 'wasn't there' and that he had to come back in four days' time to see her. The day he passed was the fourth day. Fascinating, isn't it?

I love that the deceased can give us a little sneaky advanced information about what is coming up in our lives, even if they're not really meant to.

Beautiful Blue Sky

In 1999, I 'died' from congestive heart failure. People say they see a light at the end of a tunnel. I didn't ... I saw a beautiful blue sky, like you see when you fly in an aeroplane. This voice told me (not a man or woman – it's hard to explain) my daughter was going to have a girl. So when later I'd recovered and my daughter Brandy told me she was expecting, I told her she was having a girl, even though three ultrasound scans said it was a boy.

Two weeks before the baby was born, Brandy and I had words over it. She said if I wanted a granddaughter I'd have to go to her sister and brother. You ought to have seen my daughter's face when Paige popped out ... a girl, just as 'the voice' had told me!

Ultrasound scans are great for telling the sex of a baby in advance, but they're not always correct. Luckily, in my daughter's case the prediction (backed up by her grandfather's announcement) that she was having a girl was correct. These days people rush out and buy either pink (for a girl) or blue (for a boy) items for the baby (at least in my part of the world).

LOOKING 'DEAD' GOOD

It's common for loved ones to appear younger in dream-visits than they were at the point of death. This seems to show us how well and fit our loved ones are after shedding their earthly bodies. Dad and his brother Eric both appeared to me as younger than in life, although initially Uncle Eric arrived with a balding head, which resulted in much giggling from the brothers when they appeared in their dream-visitation to me. I believe they probably thought I wouldn't recognize a younger-looking uncle.

Here is Pauline's story, which reflects the same phenomenon.

Young Again

My mother's youngest sister was my favourite auntie. We did not see much of each other, as she moved around the country a lot, but the love I felt for her never diminished. Years later she told me that I had always been her favourite niece.

Just after her 80th birthday she developed dementia. By this time she was living a three-hour drive from us and my husband, who is disabled, could no longer drive that far. As I don't drive it was very difficult for me visit her.

When she died last year I was hoping that I would feel her presence. She was psychic and so am I; I often feel that my parents and my grandmother are near, but had not sensed my auntie, and worried she might have been upset that I hadn't been to visit her.

A few months ago I had a beautiful dream. It was the sort of dream that afterwards you know wasn't just a dream. In this experience I was standing looking at some sort of view when suddenly my auntie appeared in the distance. She looked exactly like a photo I have of her when she was in her early twenties and she was dressed in the fashions of the time, just after the Second World War. She had very striking light blue eyes which I also saw clearly. It was definitely her! She ran towards me with her arms outstretched and hugged me. I recalled that I'd never known her when she was this young in life.

SECRET KNOWLEDGE

I love the stories where deceased loved ones take their living relatives on a dream-visit. Dawn experienced books in her dream which sound like the books of life (also known as the 'Akashic Records' or 'Hall of Records/Learning' – a book or a library of books which contain knowledge of all human experience). These are real places in the heavenly realms which people have described on many occasions over the years.

Book of Knowledge

My nan took me to the spirit world in my sleep to look at something in the halls of learning. She showed me some books which I already felt familiar with, and then we looked at another series of books which I was very excited about, too. I opened them and they looked as though they were written in Hebrew but I clearly understood every word.

It wasn't like a room. It was just space. It was white and all these books and information were rotating around in the air. It was magical. I saw other spirits in there, but only the 'suggestion' of a figure, glowing with pure white energy.

The books of knowledge usually describe the human journey on Earth. People are able to read about everything they have done on Earth and, bizarrely, everything they have said and thought. It makes me realize how important it is to be kind to those around us. If your every thought and deed is recorded, let's hope that one day, if we get to review our lives, we can be proud of everything we did, said and thought ...

So many accounts from my postbag contain amazing stories from the medical profession, I felt them worthy of their own chapter. I was mesmerized, and you will be, too!

Spirit Nurse

Death ... the last sleep? No, it is the final awakening.
– Sir Walter Scott

I run a lot of workshops and give talks around the country. For some reason my workshops are always full of nurses and others who care for the sick. These beautiful souls are always looking for ways of reassuring and caring for their patients, including learning about communication from the other side.

Thank goodness for nurses, but you know I also receive stories about 'spirit nurses' – nurses who no longer live in a body on this side of life, at least. It seems that the caring nature never goes away, and the bond between nurses and their patients is hard to break. Once a healer, always a healer I guess ... but more of this later.

HEAVEN'S CRADLES
Tragically, some babies never make it to this side of life, or pass over shortly after birth. I believe that new souls want to experience life on Earth for the very first time and may decide to test the waters with a short life ... they pick parents who will love them very

much, even though their visit is brief. On occasion that same soul comes back in a new body with the same family (or close family friend). When they are ready they're born again, and previously I've encountered stories that indicate this.

Our loved ones on the other side of life are taking care of these very young babies on heaven-side for us. Babies are always looked after by a spirit nurse (a soul with experience of caring for the young, or a relative, often a grandparent).

If you've ever wondered if your loved ones in heaven meet up with each other, they do. Let me reassure you, your loved ones (especially babies and children) who don't stay on this side of life are always cared for in the afterlife.

Here's Melisa's story.

A Tragedy Healed by My Angel Nanny

March 31st 1991, Easter Sunday, at 26 weeks pregnant I gave birth to my first son. I knew he would be stillborn as the hospital had had to induce me due to complications, but I was still completely heartbroken. My firstborn son was already dead.

The nurses would not allow me to see him as they said I was in no fit state to handle it. However, my husband Steve saw him and said he was beautiful. This was little consolation to me, though. The pastor came to visit next day to arrange the funeral and I named my boy Luke, from the Bible.

Luke was buried in the children's cemetery in a tiny white coffin along with some blue flowers and a teddy bear. I found it difficult to cry; I could not connect an image with my baby because I'd never even seen him. (Although I did a lot of crying in the weeks previous to his birth when I already knew he would probably die.)

A week later we had to go back to the hospital where a consultant told us that Luke had had Down's syndrome along with other complications. For months I'd had nightmares that my son was a monster, and Steve could not convince me otherwise.

Rather shockingly I found out that I was expecting again after only a month and, as you might expect, I was terrified that something would go wrong again. One evening Steve found me sitting up in bed crying; he asked me what was the matter. I told him that I'd been woken up from a deep sleep and my nanny, who'd died the year before, had brought Luke to show me. She'd placed him in my arms, where I cradled him lovingly. My baby was smiling up at me and absolutely beautiful ... not a monster at all. Nanny told me not to worry about him because she was looking after him in heaven for me. Then she lifted him back from my arms and left the room.

I don't think Steve was convinced that this actually happened to me, but it did, I know it was real. I now knew that my son was no monster but an angel and that he was being cared for, and it was really comforting.

The good news is that the following April I gave birth to a healthy 10lb son. Mediums have since told me that he is sensitive to the psychic world, like his mum, and that his brother Luke is his guardian angel.

Whilst visiting a psychic evening in Norwich, I was picked to receive a message from my mother, who had passed over in 1993. When the psychic medium spoke about my son I told her that I had never seen him when he was born, but she reminded me that I had and that he was brought to me and placed in my arms! How true she was. I was amazed that the psychic would know this.

Recently my son, now aged 18, was involved in a car accident. He told me that while he was lying in hospital he felt that he was lifted from his body and all around him he could see angels. He'd fractured ribs along with a severely bruised lung and kidney. The doctors said he was lucky to be alive.

That night I asked the angels to take away his pain, and immediately I had pain all down my right side, the side he had injured. The next morning we went to the hospital and he was out of bed ready to come home. I could not believe it; when we had left him he was on oxygen and wired up to machines. Miracles really do happen, don't they?

Melisa, England

I wonder if his guardian-angel elder brother Luke might have had a little to do with it?!

Here is another spirit helper who happens to be a relative. Who was waiting by the bed? This story came via e-mail.

Grandma at the Bed

I have just finished reading another of your inspirational books and thought I would send you a story of my own experience. In August 1996 I was suddenly taken very ill and rushed into hospital. Emergency tests showed that there was a large mass on my ovary and fallopian tube. It was so large that it was starting to cover my womb. I was told that I would need surgery the following morning, and had to sign consent forms to allow for a full hysterectomy if needed.

I was 26 years old and engaged to be married, and the thought of losing my womb and not being able to have children was devastating, but I also had to accept that there was no other way forward. I signed the papers and the next morning was prepared for surgery.

The anaesthetist came to see me and terrified me by telling me that because it was an emergency and there had been no time for me to stop taking the contraceptive pill, there could be a problem with my blood clotting and that surgery was a massive risk to my life. I was totally shocked, as was the staff nurse who had overheard the anaesthetist. The nurse escorted the anaesthetist away, and thankfully within minutes my dad was by my side to lend his support.

The surgery took place and I remember coming through a fog and feeling intense pain, so much so that I felt I could not move. I heard someone say, 'Press the button.' Instinctively I pressed my thumb against something I held in my hand. (I later knew that I was attached to a morphine drip that is administered in a measured dose by pressing a button.) Then the voice said, 'Look.' I made myself turn my head to the right and there, standing in between the two tables of flowers by my bed, was my grandmother, Granny Daisy, who had passed over when I was seven years old. She gave me the most beautiful smile and nodded her head to me before fading away. At that moment I knew that I was going to be fine; my angels were watching over me. Some people may say that the morphine was making me have hallucinations but I know she was there, reassuring me that everything was going to be OK.

Recently I was at a demonstration in a spiritualist church, and the medium connected with my Granny Daisy. During the message she said to remember when I had seen her at the hospital and that she was protecting me now just like she did then. Isn't that amazing? I have never doubted that Granny was with me that day, giving me her love, strength and support.

Helen, England

What a stressful operation Helen went through, but I'm sure she felt some comfort from her spirit visitor. Isn't it wonderful to know that our loved ones are watching out for us still? Granny Daisy, as with the story of brother Luke earlier, is acting as Helen's guardian angel from the other side.

Here is another story. Our loved ones are brilliant at bringing comfort from heaven-side ... as we've already seen. They love to show us that they are still around, and this story also has a second message. The deceased also know when we personally are ready to receive a message from them. If you're still waiting for your message then maybe you haven't had one yet because you're not ready! What does that mean? Let's have a look and see.

Not Ready?

I just wanted to share my experiences with you. My auntie Angela passed away on 10th November, 11 years ago. She was killed in a car crash. Her partner also died that day, but her baby daughter and mum (my nan) both survived, which we were all so thankful for.

It affected me very badly. I was close to her, and the thought of never seeing her again scared me. I can't remember how long it was after her death that I had a dream-visitation of her, but I remember I was dreaming that I was sitting in my nan's front room alone watching TV, although I don't recall what I was watching at the time. All of a sudden the brightest of lights shone down in front of the TV. It was an oval shape and it was so bright, but it didn't hurt my eyes. I saw my auntie in the light and I remember shouting, 'Angela, Angela!' She looked so good considering she had died that horrific way; she didn't have a scratch on her!

I ran over to her and hugged her, she said she loved me and not to worry, she was OK; I remember saying to her that my mum and nan were in the kitchen and they would love to see her! But she told me no, they weren't ready yet. So I didn't call them – after all, my Auntie Angela always knew best! Then she said she had to go. I gave her one last hug and she went. Then my nan and mum came into the room, and at that point I woke up.

I felt so happy, I was crying but they were happy tears because I knew my auntie had come to see me. She knew that I was worried and she wanted to let me know she was safe and happy.

The next dream-visitation I had of her was a few months later. My brother, who is a year older than me, was going through a bad time. He was getting into a lot of trouble and we were all concerned for him. I remember dreaming that I was sitting on a grass verge which happened to be near the cemetery where my auntie is laid to rest. I turned to my right and there she was. She looked so cool! She had her black sunglasses on and her black combats, clothes I remember her wearing in life. Her red hair looked so healthy!

She said to me she wasn't happy with Lee (my brother) and she was worried. I needed to tell him that and he would listen to her. I asked her what it was like 'up there' (heaven) and she replied 'It's like an airport, people keep checking in and out.' I told her I missed her greatly and she said she knows but I will see her again and not to worry because she hasn't 'gone' forever, it's just like she's taking a long vacation. I also knew in my head that my mum and nan were picking me up from the verge and I told her to wait a little bit so they could see her, but she said the same thing as before: that they were not ready yet. She said goodbye and went.

Then a few months later I dreamed that I was walking up the long road that leads to my nan's house when I saw my Auntie Angela again walking in the opposite direction. I called out to her and started running towards her, but a large white transit-type van appeared and she jumped in, and off they drove. I remember waking up feeling confused and upset, wondering why she hadn't spoke to me. Later that day I was talking to my nan about it and she said that the previous night she was lying in bed falling asleep when she heard the words, 'Mum, Mum,' and she knew straight away it was Angela. Nan told me she was too scared to open her eyes and look to see her (she now regrets this because Angela hasn't come back to her since).

I then realized the reason why Angela hadn't spoken to me in my dream was that she came to visit my nan that time, not me! I saw her just passing on by. I then felt better knowing she had a reason for ignoring me.

Another time I also had a dream-visit from my gran. I remember being in a large old mansion. I was sitting in one of the bedrooms and there was a large dressing table with a mirror opposite me. I felt my gran's presence and started talking to her. She never showed herself in that room but her hands appeared to me. Then she started kissing another person's hands, and even though I didn't see the other person I knew they were Mum's hands.

I was then led down a long corridor. This time I was holding my gran's hand. I could now see her clearly, but she was her young self. I use to say to her when she was here that she looked so much like the actress Marilyn Monroe! She was stunning as a young woman. It's like she showed herself to me in that way because she knew how beautiful I thought she looked.

Gran led me to the end of the corridor and in front of a large door. She opened the door and in the middle of a large room was my granddad, her husband who had passed many years before her. He was showing himself as his young self, too. He was a handsome young sailor. I used to be amazed at how handsome he was, too, so it was lovely to see them in this way.

My gran smiled at me and let go of my hand and walked towards her husband, then they held hands and started dancing to a song which I only vaguely remembered. It was called 'We'll Meet Again.' Then they went. When I woke I told my mum, who told me it had been their favourite song!

The last dream I had of my auntie was recently, just a few weeks ago. I've been reading your books, and have so many mixed emotions. I've also been very distressed lately because I've been thinking about my son who passed away. As most parents do, I was wondering if he's safe and well, wondering if I'm ever going to see him again, etc. I felt guilty when he passed over because even though I was allowed to spend some time with him, when the nurse came in to take him I just handed him over, without kicking and screaming or making a fuss. It was like I was in a trance. He passed away in my arms at the hospital. We had called for the hospital chaplain to help him cross over. My mum, stepdad and partner were all present at the time as well.

One night I dreamt that I was in the same scenario: I was sitting in the same chair and I was holding my baby boy, I was crying and the others around me were. The chaplain was reading prayers. Everything was exactly how it was the day he passed, except one thing: Aunt Angela was there. She was standing at my right shoulder, waiting patiently. I could feel her lovely safe presence next to me. When my baby Harvey passed over, I knew that I had to hand him over to Angela, so I turned to my right and she had her arms out ready. As I handed him over she smiled at me before walking towards a bright light, and they both disappeared into it.

When I woke I felt so happy. It was like she had come to show me she had come to collect Harvey when he'd died – it was such a relief! I knew then that he was safe and well, and that he wasn't alone.

I'd had many nightmares that he was alone and I was scared that he would get lost. I even got a plot in the cemetery right next to my auntie and grandparents rather than have him be in the baby section all alone. After that dream I still feel guilty that I handed him over to the nurse that day, but I now feel more at ease.

When Aunt Angela died she had a baby girl. Olivia is now 11 and is the image of her mum. My mum adopted her, no questions asked, and I helped my mum to raise her, even though I was only young myself. I felt Angela came to collect Harvey and to let me know she had him as a way of saying thank you, and returning the 'favour'.

Sometimes these dreams scare me, because they can be about deaths in the family. And obviously you don't want your loved one to die. But I remember the comfort they can bring, too. If our loved ones have to go, at least we can still see them again in some way.

Jade, England

Guilt is a symptom of grief. We feel guilty for the silliest of reasons after the loss of a loved one (for more information about this, see my book *Angels Watching Over Me*, also published by Hay House). Of course Jade had nothing whatsoever to feel guilty about.

Auntie Angela sounds amazing! Not many spirits have the ability to appear to loved ones over and over again like this ... she sounds practised at afterlife communication in the way my own late father is! Imagine the comfort Jade felt when she knew her dear son was safely being taken care of. What a blessing. Many people long for such clear signs; if only they could all appear in this way. The good news is that these dream-visitations are becoming more frequent, so if you haven't had a dream-visitation yet, you might still.

CALLING ANGELS TO THE BEDSIDE OF THE SICK

Of course, our angels are already at the bedside of the sick – maybe a better heading would be, 'giving our angels permission to help us'? Your own guardian angel is always close by and we each have our own guardian angel. I'll keep repeating that to remind you. You are always supported and loved at all times.

Angels are needed in many situations on Earth, including bereavement. Bad news, especially a death, can literally cause physical symptoms, real pain. If you've experienced this yourself then you'll already know what I am talking about: emotional pain really does hurt in a physical way. Angels can assist in situations like this by bringing physical healing ... those loving angel arms can soothe the ache, as many readers have written to tell me all about.

As usual you don't need any special tricks to ask that this be done – simply ask your angel (in your head ... or write it down if you wish). You only need to say HELP and they will. If you feel that a ritual or meditation will help you more, then you're right, it will. Here are a few ideas, for you or to pass on to a friend.

HEALING ANGEL-BATH

Take a bath in warm water (a comfortable heat for you, which will vary from person to person) – the temperature is 'relaxing-heat'! Light a couple of candles if you wish or play some soothing angelic-type music ... whatever calms you. Make sure the room is warm enough and maybe treat yourself to some new bath products, slippers or robe. I want you to feel pampered!

As you relax in the bath, imagine that the water is healing angel light ... you can ask that your angels pour their energy into the water at the same time as the warmth soothes your body. Let your mind create this image for you – feel it for real. Relax for as long as you can (or as long as you feel comfortable/are warmed by the water). I want you to imagine that the soothing warmth is coming from your guardian angel.

The physical warmth of the water will help you to relax into the right state of mind, to feel and experience your angels close by your side ... there is no reason why you can't actually feel the angels pulling close.

If you don't like baths, have a shower ... you can sit on a plastic chair in the shower so that you can relax for as long as you need. If you need help, wait until someone is around to lift a safe plastic chair into the shower (following safely guidelines) … putting your back out is NOT relaxing!

Sitting in a hot tub (jacuzzi/spa bath), if you are lucky enough to have access to one, can be a fantastic relaxation/angel experience, too … maybe a trip to a local spa is a possibility as a special treat? The bubbles will also relax you and help you to feel your angels close by. It works every time. Hot tubs are my favourite meditation place! It's also where I get my best ideas. During the relaxation of this exercise I feel my angels draw really close, and you will, too.

HEALING FOODS … WITH A LITTLE ANGELIC SUPPORT

The angels are always asking people to look after their diet. I'm not talking about 'diet' as in losing weight, but diet as in what food you put in your mouth. It's challenging to change the way you eat – especially changing the types of foods you eat. My weight has gone up and down over the years, as I have made changes successfully and then slipped back into the old eating patterns. I know a LOT of my readers will relate to this!

Doctors believe that some of the foods we are allergic to are the ones we crave the most … particularly sugar. I am not a doctor but I can tell you from my own experience that cutting down (and giving up) sugar made me a different person: I was clearer in my head, physically lighter and mentally more psychic. Yes, I felt more attuned to my angels and more … bouncy! OK, that sounds a little nutty, but what I mean is that I had more physical energy and did everything at a faster speed. I enjoyed life more and felt healthier.

Yes, I made mistakes and began eating sugar again … it's a craving, an addiction, a little like alcohol and cigarettes, but I've stopped eating it again and I am working with a health professional this time. No one can make big life changes without support …

I've mentioned this before but the angels tell me it's time to do it again. These are the preferred foods (you have to make your own choices, of course):

- vegetables – all sorts, all colours (for a variety of vitamins)
- salads – again, a big variety of different types
- fruits – try and eat some fruit every day (though don't overdo it, because fruit can contain a lot of sugar, too)
- fruit juices (same as above)
- nuts
- seeds
- water
- good oils (like olive oil)
- fish (especially oily fish)
- lean meat (just a little – go for quality rather than quantity).

Make sure you work with a professional (dietician, doctor, etc. to eat foods which are suitable for your body). Cut right down on processed foods, sugar and animal fats. Working with an expert and checking on the internet for more information is best; a book on healthy eating (food science does change from time to time) is also a great idea. Invest in YOU. The rewards are great:

- brighter skin
- less body fat
- higher energy levels
- clearer mind
- … and my favourite: greater intuition/psychic ability … if you're lucky.

As with all things, ask your guardian angel to support you in your quest for better health. Many conditions are improved with a better diet … ask your angels to help lead you to better choices. The planet is changing and so must we. If you (like me) have food 'challenges', work to correct them, and if you fail (or if you have failed in the past) go right back and start again (and again and again). You owe it to yourself to be the best that you can be. Look after your body … take care of your health. Help the angels to help YOU.

ANGEL HEALING MEDITATION

Most meditations ask you to sit down (either on the floor or in a chair) but this one is different because I want you to lie down. If you can, lie on your bed for this exercise. Make sure the room is warm and comfortable, close the door if you need to for privacy but let other members of the household know what you are up to so you get a few minutes to yourself. You can record your own voice reading the words out loud to some relaxing music in the background, or ask a friend to read this passage to you – or simply memorize the exercise.

Don't worry if you fall asleep – allow yourself to wake up naturally when you are ready. The exercise will still work. Have a hot drink ready for when you've finished. Imagination is key. Enjoy yourself as you 'see' in your mind's eye all the things described in complete detail …

You are lying down in the penthouse suite of your luxury hotel waiting for a healing treatment. Your healer is just preparing the scented ointments and lotions. You are wearing soft and silky robes which are perfect for this treatment. They are comfortable and attractive.
Visualize this.

Everything is wonderful and beautiful. You are in this lovely place because you deserve to be here. Your hotel is right on the beach and the window is open. Visualize this before you go on.

You can hear the sound of the waves gently moving in and out ... in and out. Listen to the sound for a few moments and, as you do so, you become more and more relaxed.

Your healer has now moved in close and you know at once it's your guardian angel. Your angel wanted to create this special spa-type healing for you ... you deserve this treatment. Hear the waves ... slowly, slowly.

In ... and out, more and more relaxed.

In ... and out, more and more relaxed.

The soothing sound of the waves relaxes every part of your body ... inside, and outside ... .in and out, in and out, more and more relaxed. More and more relaxed ... relax, relax, relax.

Your angel is now by your side. Even though your eyes are closed you become aware of a beautiful glowing light of rainbow colours – this light now surrounds your entire body. Your angel is using this rainbow of light to align your energy centres. Like the conductor of an orchestra, your angel moves the light around your body, directing each colour to where it needs to go ... you may hear the beautiful sounds the colours make as they fall into alignment. Spend time enjoying the treatment. Feel the colours individually as they whirl around. Know that they are being properly aligned in a healthy and healing way.

The treatment immediately begins to make you feel well and healthy, more and more relaxed ... and all the while you hear the sound of the surf ... in ... and out ... in ... and out ...

Relax while your angel treatment is in progress. Enjoy the sensations and gentle warmth of the breeze as it blows through the open window. Feel reassured by the occasional sound of laugher on the beach below ... people having fun and enjoying life.

You are in the perfect place at the perfect time ... enjoy your treatment ... this is your special time. Know that, all the while, your angel is adding special lotions and treatments into your aura ... some people may even smell the wonderful scents of the angel-etheric treatments. Your angels just seem to know what scents are perfect for you.

Enjoy ...

Enjoy ...

[Give yourself a few minutes here, as long as you like ... listen to the relaxing music you have set up to play in the background.]

When you are ready ... you will feel your angel begin to pull away from you. Your angel spa treatment has finished. Your angel (male or female) is quietly collecting together the equipment and just fades quietly away.

You feel refreshed and well and ready to face what the world brings to you. Have a stretch if you need one. Open your eyes and bring your consciousness back into the room ... take your time and, when you are fully back, sit up slowly. Have a sip of the drink you prepared earlier (maybe waiting in a Thermos flask).

Take the opportunity of doing this meditation exercise when you need to relax rather than when you need to be very awake and alert ... it's a shame to waste all your efforts. Just before bedtime is a great time to perform this exercise, and as I mentioned before, don't worry if you fall asleep – you already know what's going to happen in the exercise (assuming you've read it through a couple of times before you start). Just know that it will still happen even if you fall asleep. Remember that during the exercise you are in control at all times and can open your eyes and stop the meditation. You will be perfectly safe at all times.

Through the Looking Glass

Once more she found herself in the long hall, and ... among the bright flower-beds and the cool fountains ...
– Alice's Adventures in Wonderland

Wouldn't it be great to know what happens when we go to heaven? What happens on the other side of life? Where do we go when we die? What do we see? What do we feel?

Millions of people have experienced what we call a near-death experience. This might be because they were physically close to death, but sometimes people experience paranormal phenomena due to bumps on the head, an expectation of death or just a physical trauma to the body. These experiences give us a clue to what real death might be like.

Near Death on a Trampoline

I was ten years old and my parents had bought me a trampoline for doing well in an exam. It was a nice morning and my friend had stayed over the night before; my mum had said we couldn't play on the trampoline until she got out of bed to supervise us. Kids being kids, we decided to sneak out anyway. I tried to do a tricky manoeuvre and failed. I ended up banging the side of my head on the metal bar and knocking myself unconscious.

When I was unconscious it felt like a tunnel of multi-coloured light was flashing towards me … it's hard to explain, bear with me … there was a silhouette of a man standing there and he was talking (I'm not sure if he was talking to me, or someone else). Being a ten-year-old you would have thought I'd have been freaked out by the experience, but I wasn't scared, more curious.

I truly believe that I was going to die that day and my guardian angel, the man, brought me back because it was not my time to go. When I regained consciousness my friend was standing over me and I immediately ran into the bathroom and threw up. I don't remember much after that but my mum took me to hospital in case I'd got concussion. I was fine.

Jenni, Northern Ireland

Jenni is not alone; it's quite common to be greeted at death's door. Angels, spirit guides and deceased relatives are among this worthy collection of heaven-side helpers. Jenni's phrase 'not your time' does pop up over and over again in these scenarios. Sometimes we're given a choice at the heavenly gates: leave with the angel who escorts you, or go back to Earth to finish your life.

THE 'DEATH' EXPERIENCE

I put the word 'death' in inverted commas because I don't believe we die in the way we traditionally think we do. Death is something that happens to the physical body. The spirit lives on.

I asked a whole stack of people on my Facebook page about death and dying experiences. It's not something that we normally talk about, yet not all death is frightening. Here are the results:

Jeannie

'When my ex-husband's uncle was dying he kept brushing the bed with his hands as if pushing something off ... "Get the water off," he kept saying. When the Macmillan nurse came she said she had seen this sort of thing often and believed that it's as if we cross an expanse of water when we're crossing over to the other side of life.'

[This is true because sometimes people see a bridge as the boundary between the Earth and heaven sides of life.]

Wendy

'I sat with my grandmother when she passed over. She knew her time had come and the sadness in her face was immense, yet she never said anything. I brushed her hair for her, put some moisturizer on her face and gave her a hand massage; then she just slipped away. It was a sad yet very beautiful experience.'

[There is that phrase again – this time Wendy's grandmother recognized that it was her time.]

Amanda

'I only met my boyfriend's grandfather twice, but it's amazing how we can connect to people in just a few meetings. I went to the hospital when he was in a coma; he seemed to just be sleeping very peacefully. I felt drawn to hold his hand and I told him, in my mind, not to be frightened and not to feel bad about leaving loved ones behind. I told him it was his time now and to go and enjoy being with his wife again.

'On the way home I couldn't shake off this strong connection, but by the next day I felt peaceful and calm. Then during lunch I felt suddenly drained of energy and thought I was going to pass out. I went to the bathroom and washed my face with cold water (this was at 12 o'clock) and I knew instinctively that my boyfriend's grandfather had passed over. When I came out of the bathroom, the phone rang: he'd died at 12 o'clock, just as I thought.

It was a beautiful experience (maybe a little scary, like giving birth): scary but special all at the same time.'

[What a great way to explain the death process! Death is a new birth, just as Amanda suggests.]

Susan

'I was unconscious; everything was white and everyone was dressed in white; they looked like doctors trying to save me. Wherever I was it was a nice place; I may have been what you could call clinically dead, but it was like nothing I've ever experienced before, even in dreams.

'Being a nurse I have seen many people pass on, and as far as I am aware they have a pleasant transition and actually feel their soul leaving the body. I do actually believe that someone from the other side appears to pick us up.'

[... and of course, Susan is right. I have hundreds of case histories where loved ones talk to those coming to collect them and escort them heaven-side ... or escort them back from the brink of death!]

Tracey

'When my nanny died my dad was sitting with her. She was really weak and was slowly getting weaker day by day. When she passed over she sat bolt upright in the bed, smiled at one corner of the room and sank back down on the bed and died peacefully. Later when we went to see a medium she said my nan's brother Joey had come to get her and that's why she was smiling.

'My dad died three years ago. In his last few days he kept trying to get out of the bed on the window side, as if he was going to "the light". The night before he died I said to my boyfriend, "He's going soon." I just knew. About 6 that morning the night nurse came up and told us he was very poorly. My mother got there first and kept saying, "Hang on, they're coming," meaning me and my brother. When I got in the room, my mother was holding his hand. My brother had his hand on Dad's leg and when I came in I put my hand on his head and in that instant he went. It was so moving he went so peacefully.'

[When people who've been previously unconscious or too ill to sit up suddenly do so in their final few moments, you know something magical is going on, especially when they point, smile or talk to unseen visitors.]

Christine

'The whole family were at the house when my mother-in-law died. We used to pop into her bedroom from time to time; it was a very long day and I felt we were keeping her from going to the other side.

'Her last few breaths were for her children and husband; it was a lovely moment but all very sad because she'd suffered a terrible illness (cancer). When my father-in-law passed over nine months later, he died in his sleep. We found him the next day in bed with all his clothes on and it looked like he knew he was going. It seems that we all felt it at the time: he didn't want to be here any more.'

[It's comforting when the dying are ready to go. Sometimes it can be easier if the illness has been a long one and the physical body is tired and ready to pass on.]

Sylvia

'I was sat with my husband in hospital when he passed over. I was holding his hand and it was my son who came in and said, 'Mum, he's gone now.' I didn't know as he was lying there so peaceful like he'd just gone to sleep but forever. When I left the room I did look up and said 'Will see you darling, when it's my time.'

[I think most of us wish that we could pass over in this gentle way ... when it's our time, of course!]

Christine

'Before my dad passed he told me that his brother-in-law had visited him in spirit. My dad even dreamt of his own funeral.'

[We know who collected this man!]

Lisa

'Just before my granddad passed in 2004 he told me that there were three men at the end of his bed in suits and that they had come to collect him. They'd told him they were waiting for him to say his "goodbyes" to his loved ones. A few hours later my granddad died, and I feel that perhaps these men were somehow "men in waiting".'

[They may have been old friends or simply this gentleman's spirit guides.]

Trudie
'When I was working as a nurse I saw many people pass over and so many of them held their hands out as if they were trying to take someone's hand ...'
[Indeed, we know they did.]

Julie's account is a long one but I have left it in full. It includes both 'announcing' experiences and an amazing afterlife visit. I know you will find it as fascinating as I did myself when I read it.

Julie
When I was working through my nursing career I had lots of experiences of being with patients when they passed over. They always seemed to wait until I was on duty when they passed. I didn't believe in people being on their own and I was always being told off for sitting with them because there was work to be done!

One unconscious patient just sat bolt upright, smiled at her family, held her arms up, looked up at the ceiling and then passed. When they were close to their time I found that patients would talk incessantly to beings that the rest of us could not see. One said to me that she could see her family waiting on a steam train and she kept trying to throw her blanket up to them so they wouldn't get cold because they had been waiting for days!

Another woman in a nursing home was found getting her belongings ready. I asked her what she was doing and she told me that she was getting ready because at 8 p.m. her 'husband' was coming to collect her. During the afternoon she got herself dressed (I helped her) and as the time got close she was so excited. At 8 p.m. she was on the end of her bed smiling, with her coat on! Considering she was normally unable to dress herself, this must have taken quite an effort.

Not surprisingly, the woman died at 8 p.m.; I checked her pulse and she had gone. The last I had seen of her was at 7:45 and she was talking to her husband then looking up at the ceiling all the time and smiling. She was thanking him for waiting for her to get ready and for coming to get her like he said he would.

Unfortunately I was occupied with another patient at the moment she passed ... I so wanted to be with her at 8 p.m. I believe she was not alone anyway, bless her. A couple of the other nurses didn't believe her, and thought it was her dementia talking, but I just knew that she was telling the truth. She and her husband had both lived in the nursing home together; they had been missionaries together throughout their lives, so they had faith anyway. He was a lovely man, and she was a real dear. She looked so peaceful, sat with her shoes on and her coat, and her handbag in her hand. She even had a little lipstick on ...

I loved my work in nursing homes; there is just something about older people I find fascinating. I felt extremely honoured that the patients chose to go when I was with them. I would always make sure I was around them. Some people found it morbid but I felt excited at the role. One woman who usually spoke to no one looked me straight in the eyes just before she passed away and said, 'I am going to a much better place, I know exactly who you are, Julie, and I really appreciate you looking after me and caring. The place I'm going is peaceful and my brother is waiting for me. There is nothing left here now, thank you.' Just then a nurse walked in and my patient went quiet and never spoke again. As usual, no one believed me!

I have always felt connected to the afterlife. When I was 12 my gran sent me a message in a dream telling me she was going to die (no pictures, just words). Her message was, 'I'm going to die soon,' and then I heard my own voice saying, 'No you're not, you're going to live until you're a hundred ... a hundred ... a hundred.'

Then my mum knocked on my bedroom door and woke me to say, 'I've got to go, love, Gran's been taken ill.' Gran did die then, just as she'd told me in my dream.

Another day I was taken on a wonderful journey with my spiritual guide who introduced herself and took me to see Gran. We were flying up through the clouds and I could even feel my stomach lurching as if I were on a fairground ride. I recall the sky was the brightest blue I have ever seen. My guide showed me the hospitals where souls go if they die suddenly and need healing.

I was shown fields of beautiful green pastures and lots of buttercups and daisies, but they were brighter colours than I have ever seen before. She took me to this beautiful cottage where my gran was sat with a pot of tea waiting for me. I asked my gran why she was drinking tea when she was in heaven, because it seemed a strange thing to do, and she explained that if you die suddenly then you are able to enjoy some of the earthly home comforts for a while as you adjust, even though you don't need them any more.

Also out in the garden of the cottage she had lions roaming around, tigers and normal cats and dogs (we both loved animals). I said, 'What's going on? Won't they hurt each other?' Gran explained that all animals live in harmony in heaven; they have no need to kill each other because they don't need food any more. It was amazing.

Next I was taken to visit a schoolteacher of mine who had died of cancer. She was bald when I'd last seen her but she had gorgeous long flowing blonde hair in heaven. Eventually I had to leave. I was told to lie down with my hands across my chest and that I would wake up like that. Sure enough I did wake up with my arms folded in that way, but I was also paralysed for quite a while as I lay in bed. I could not move or cry out, even though I tried. When my cat saw me she hissed and her hair stood on end.

I can remember it now as clearly as if it had happened yesterday. Anyway, I have to say, it feels so good to write these things down knowing that you understand what I am talking about and believe me. Over the years when I've chosen to open up to people they just don't believe what I'm saying. I suppressed my experiences for years, for fear of ridicule!

I've heard of trains being shown as a sign of transport in 'escorting' dreams previously – and in fact had a train dream a little like this myself. I'm not sure that there are trains in heaven ... Although I could be wrong, I'm sure these things are displayed to us in these ways so that we can understand what is happening. Some of Julie's heaven-visit experiences are similar to others I've read about. And Julie ... of course it's real! I believe you.

Medical staff seem to have extraordinary experiences relating to passing over. It's quite a privilege to be with someone when they actually cross over, but sitting with some patients can delay the inevitable as they try and 'hold on' to please us. (They can't delay forever so don't feel guilty if you've sat with the dying – we don't have *that* much influence ... only when it's not that person's time to go, in which case I believe we can encourage them back into the body. People who've experienced near-death do often recall a voice – sometimes familiar – calling them back ... although it's just as likely to be a spirit on the other side pushing them back into their body!).

When my own father died in the hospital our family had all just popped out for lunch. He had a heart attack and died during that short break we took, yet we'd literally spent years sitting by his hospital bedside following him around to different hospitals around the world, taking it in turns to sit by his bed so he was rarely alone ... even when it wasn't normal visiting hours.

I really believe that what happens, happens and there is nothing we can do about it. Maybe the dying just sometimes require a little privacy to begin their special journey! Of course, as our stories show, our loved ones are NEVER completely alone and are always collected, either by angels, spiritual guides, deceased relatives and pets or all of these together ... and there are thousands and thousands of real-life stories to prove it!

This amazing story is one where someone took a wonderful trip to the afterlife just like Julie did. It's rare but, as we've already seen, it does happen. Personally I long to visit heaven-side, but naturally I don't want to have to go through an illness or accident to get there. Maybe a loved one or guide will take me on a little visit, too? Here's Angela's experience.

A Trip to Heaven

I had such an amazing dream some time ago, which seemed so real and, even now a few years later, I can clearly remember every detail of the experience. I was sitting in a kind of waiting room. Another person was present and then someone came to fetch him and I was left on my own. While I was sitting there I felt completely at ease and very calm. Within a short time someone came to fetch me, too. Although the person was standing next to me I could not see his or her face. The facial area seemed blurry but that didn't seem to bother me at the time.

The person was taller than me and slim, wearing a light-coloured outfit. Again it seemed blurry and although I could clearly hear the voice, it was more in my head than spoken in the normal way. I couldn't tell you if this person was male or female (it didn't seem relevant). Next I was taken into a very large hall where there seemed to be an audience sitting in front of a pulpit. In the pulpit stood a very tall man; I believed this man was a type of angel. He was dressed in a gold gown and was addressing the audience. Behind him were a lot of people and they seemed to be smiling and excited. They were pointing to members of the audience and some of the audience were waving to them. My guide, as I will refer to him, told me that they had recognized their loved ones in the congregation. He later said that he would show me around, and we walked down some long white corridors. Along one of the corridors was a very large window and through it I could see the sky. I was amazed at this, and said that I didn't think there would be a sky here. It was the most beautiful sky that I have ever seen. The colours were blue, lilac and pink – so vivid, like sunset colours.

My guide took me outside where there was a lovely calm sea in a bay. People were swimming or just standing in the water. My guide asked me to follow him as he walked out into the water, but I was reluctant because I am afraid of deep water. He reassured me that I would be OK because no matter how far I went out to sea it would only come up to my chest, so I followed him.

We both stood in the water watching the other people enjoying the experience, but I noticed a man who was limping. I turned to my guide and asked why he was limping and his reply, his exact words were, 'He hasn't adjusted yet, he is still clinging on to his earthly life. When he adjusts he will lose the limp.' I then said that if I was experiencing death then I wondered why everyone seemed afraid even though I wasn't, but I never got my answer because I woke up.

Angela, England

More beautiful flowers, gorgeous colours and swimming in the sea – it sounds wonderful, doesn't it? Can you imagine if heaven were easy for everyone to visit in this way? You just make a request and then when you go to sleep you go and buy your ticket, wait for your turn and then just have a guided tour. Thankfully some people do have these experiences so we can follow along.

After my father passed over my daughter's boyfriend had a dream-visitation in which my dad popped in to say hello. Kyle told me that during the experience he saw the most wonderful sky with rainbow colours ... he said it was beautiful and unlike anything he had ever seen before. I'm starting to notice a bit of a theme here, aren't you?

When people are privileged enough to sit with the dying, they sometimes experience similar things to that which the dying feel themselves. This might include: lights, sounds, smells and in particular wonderful colours, as in the previous story. We've already looked at people holding out their arms to their angels and loved ones heaven-side, now let's have a look at some new encounters.

Beautiful Death

It had been weeks since I'd realized my son of seven would not recover from the cancer he was diagnosed with some seven months earlier; over that time much of it was spent living on the ward along with other parents going through similar harrowing times.

Jamie had been a typical seven-year-old, causing mischief and mayhem wherever he went; very much Daddy's boy. Over a matter of months he was basically bedridden, although he could often be found riding his drip-stand down the ward like it was a scooter.

One night I'd managed to get him on my lap and as I sat on his bed with tears streaming down my cheeks, hugging him as I'd never hugged him before, I was praying for him to go peacefully in his sleep. That following morning (Remembrance Sunday) at 6 a.m. he passed away. The nurse had woken me a few minutes before to say he was going and I'd scrambled to my feet and made it to his bedside just as a beautiful light filled the room. The scent of flowers also filled the room and a nurse commented on how peaceful the room was. For some reason it didn't feel like the sterile room it really was. The bright lights, although they were pale colours

127

of red, yellow, green, blue and purple, appeared to have what I can only describe as glitter thrown into the colour and it seemed to flow around the room. I felt a warmth and comfort as though I was being physically held, but I wasn't, not by any human anyway. This feeling stayed with me for a long while until members of my family and my husband got there. I had two other children at home so my husband was with them at home. My daughter knew her brother had died because she said that fairy lights had come into her room and she felt at peace.

I still don't know where my strength came from that day and for a long time afterwards. I like to think it was the angels.

Paula, England

Paula herself called the experience a 'beautiful death' so I have used this as the title of her story. Tragic though this experience is, I know that Paula did receive some small comfort at the point of Jamie's death. Isn't it magical that Jamie's sister saw the glittery lights whilst she was at home? It's as if she too were sharing the passing-over scene.

Death at any age is so heartbreaking, but once the soul has left the body its heavenly journey is a peaceful one. Suffering is something that happens to those left behind and there are many stories of 'near-death' which indicate the passage that we go through at the time of crossing over. Of course people who experience near-death don't die, but they're sometimes privileged to have that tiny glimpse of the magic of the other side of life …

I always find stories of heaven to be very fascinating – who doesn't want to know what happens next and where we go? Here is another near-death experience where the person found herself in the heavenly hospital when leaving the body. Naturally she made an earthly recovery and so returned to her human body to share the experience, but one assumes that if she hadn't she could have stayed in this heaven-side hospital until ready to move on as spirit.

Heaven's Hospitals

I was drifting gently off to sleep when I felt like I had risen out of my body. I opened my eyes to find I was hovering above my body, which I could still feel was resting. Next I shot off at a million miles a second and I was in a kind of hospital, but everyone who was there had already died and this was the place for their spirit to heal from their earthly ills.

There were a few others like me, but they were from Earth and they were nurses. One of them called me over by calling me 'sister'. I looked at this stranger and drew a blank; I did not answer her because I did not know her. She looked at me kind of funny and smiled before telling everyone to carry on without me; she realized I wasn't quite with them ... not yet! I know it sounds completely strange.

There were also women in the hospital who had passed during childbirth, some with the child also. It was so sad.

I'm going into so much detail I know, yet this happened over seven years ago before I fell pregnant with my third son. I have visited other areas of the hospital at different times, as well as what I call the 'halfway house'. It's kind of like a hotel for those who don't know what to do or where to go, and to help deal with their passing slowly. I know I sound like a complete nut job but I've had these experiences several times

now. If you have any idea what this is all about I would be
interested as to what you make of my 'odd' experiences.

Janette, England

I do have an idea, Janette! The hospital scenario appears over and
over again, as do variations on the 'halfway house' (a little like the
gran drinking tea in her cottage – she too was adjusting to life on
the other side).

Afterlife expert and hypnotherapist Dr Michael Newton, in
his book *Journey of Souls*, describes these hospital-type locations.
Many of my readers will have heard me quoting his work before.
Dr Newton uses hypnosis to talk to his clients about past lives
and lives between lives. After regressing subjects using deep
hypnotic trance sessions he is able to ask many questions about
what happens in heaven. Many clients mention a place, or space of
healing. Some go through a type of healing shower of light; others
find themselves in a hospital-type setting as Janette did.

Isn't it a comfort to know that after a long earthly illness, when
we pass over our souls are healed before we carry on? The deep
aches and pains of the soul are washed clean.

Mandy didn't know she was dying when she had her experience
… it's a good job her husband was on hand to bring her back to
life. Here is Mandy's letter:

The Place Where Children Laugh

I've been reading your books for some time now in the hope
of reading something similar to what I experienced some
years ago myself. It would be about 18 years ago now that
I passed out because of a really bad stomach ache. This is
something that had happened to me before … and since, but

on this occasion I managed to call my husband just before it happened, knowing that I was going to pass out.

What happened next is something that my husband explained to me after the event. He came into the bathroom and I'd apparently fallen and swallowed my tongue! He says he found me on the floor making a gurgling sound. He told me he'd never been so frightened in his whole life; my face looked like a 'death face', apparently. He had to put his fingers in my mouth to pull my tongue out of the back of my throat!

All I remember of the incident is actually something that still stays with me even today. Whilst all this was happening I felt an indescribable feeling of annoyance at having been woken from the most wonderful 'dream'. I remember the delightful sound of children's laughter and immense love.

It's hard to put into words the annoyance I felt at being 'brought back'. If you imagine the most wonderful dream you've ever had, multiply it by 10, and then imagine getting woken up and multiply that feeling of annoyance by 50, this is probably close to the feeling I had.

It was late in the evening when this happened so it definitely wasn't the sound of children outside or anything. All the stories I read about are of people seeing bright lights or loved ones. I didn't see anything, just felt the wonderful feeling of love and heard the sound of children's laughter. I really think I experienced some kind of out-of-body experience and 'something' spirit-side? If this is the feeling you get when you cross over, then I'm in no way frightened of when it will be my time. The feeling was absolutely wonderful, which is why I was so annoyed at being woken up.

Mandy, England

Many years ago I was staying at my parents' house and fell asleep. Whilst I was asleep I experienced something similar to Mandy. I felt this wonderful overwhelming sense of love and peace and was happy to stay in this state of consciousness forever. Imagine how annoyed I was when I heard Mum calling me and asking me if I wanted a cup of tea. I woke up and that wonderful feeling drifted away at once. Bizarrely I soon discovered that Mum and Dad were sound asleep in the other room ... I believe my guardian angels had tricked me to get me to come back to this side of life!

Here's another story of someone passing over once they were alone:

No Taxis

My nan passed away in December 2000. She had pancreatic cancer, and in the last few days of her life she was kept heavily sedated. My mum and my aunt were sat with Nan for much of this time, and have both told me that, despite the sedation, Nan had several episodes where she was unsettled, tossing and turning and talking to someone that neither my mum nor my aunt could see. Much of what my nan said was difficult to understand, but my mum and aunt both said it sounded as though Nan was arguing with someone and insisting that she wasn't going, she wasn't going ... Mum also thought she heard Nan say the name 'Cyril', which was my granddad's name.

About two days after this happened for the last time, my mum and aunt had both left my nan's bedside to go home to get some clean clothes. They both checked with her consultant that she would be OK overnight, and my uncle was to return the next morning. My aunt left first as she had to get from the south coast to Yorkshire, and mum left later as she had a shorter journey to make. From subsequent conversations it was established that Mum had got in shortly after my aunt. Ten minutes later the phone rang: it was the hospital, saying Nan had passed 'in the last 5 minutes'. As they knew Mum, my aunt and my uncle were too far away to get back quickly, they had phoned my great-aunt (Nan's sister) when Nan took a turn for the worse. My great-aunt was unable to get to the hospital as none of the local taxi firms had any cabs spare.

It always seems strange that Nan died so soon after Mum (the last of her three children) got home safely and that there were no taxis available for her sister to visit, either.

We always wondered if it was my granddad's influence that affected the timing of her passing; it was as if he knew Nan wouldn't go with him until everyone was home, so he made sure everyone was at home so that he could take her with him!

Amy, England

Unconscious Helper

Do all the good you can, and make as
little fuss about it as possible.
– Charles Dickens

OUT-OF-BODY TRAVELLERS

Now, one minute you're lying in bed minding your own business and the next you're floating on the ceiling ... I'm serious! Maybe you're rocking backwards and forwards, or perhaps you're just floating above your body, either looking at the ceiling or face-down looking at your body. It happens all the time and mostly people put it down to being a strange (but very real) dream.

I had several out-of-body experiences a few years ago ... you can do it on purpose using various deep meditation techniques but you have to practise. I would sometimes find my spirit body floating around the house or elsewhere. Many people around the world have experienced out-of-body phenomena. Your spiritual self (your personality) splits from your physical body and your consciousness remains with it. There are famous stories of this being witnessed by others; in fact, an old friend of mine woke to find her 'secret' boyfriend standing at the end of the bed. The two of them had spent an illicit evening together and didn't want to part ... it seems their spirits didn't, either, because when she looked more closely, the 'body' of her boyfriend disappeared ... it had been only his spirit that had visited.

Angels often visit us when we sleep or when we are unconscious. I remember my dad once 'flew' all the way from the hospital to my home, and when I saw him next he was able to describe everything he had seen. Yes – by flew I mean he was in his 'spiritual body' rather than using a personal plane! He was doing what we call flying 'out of body', most commonly called an 'out-of-body experience'.

Out-of-body experiences are surprisingly common and can happen when people are close to death or very ill, but also when the body is tired or restless. Some people have experienced OBE when they simply thought they were going to die ... the spirit being literally scared out of the body. It can also happen by accident, when the body is suddenly jolted. I've never discovered any negative effects of out-of-body travel.

Dad was ill when he had his own out-of-body flight, just three months away from his own passing. As he got closer to his death he became more fluid within his body. This particular evening he was all alone in his hospital room and restless. Knowing that I had an interest in all things paranormal, I guess I was the first daughter of choice for a visit.

The first time my sister Debbie had this experience she blamed me ... well, we had previously spoken about out-of-body experiences and she felt that in talking about the phenomenon I had somehow prompted her own encounter (if only it were that simple!). Debbie suddenly awoke, but not in her physical body –

Debbie was rocking backwards and forwards in her astral (spirit) body! Has this ever happened to you? Drinking too much alcohol can cause a similar experience (but not in a good way). Have you ever walked up the stairs when you were drunk and felt that the rest of your body was slow to follow, resulting in a sort of rocking motion? The walls seem to move as you stand still (not nice though really, is it?).

Here is a flying 'dream' that is really an out-of-body experience. Sounds crazy? Read on.

Practice Run-through

As my friend didn't drive she asked me if I would drive her to meet her parents in the countryside (Bundernoon NSW) for the weekend. It was a trip I had never been on before so my friend suggested she bring a map for me the following day.

Rather strangely and unexpectedly, I had a disturbed night including a very helpful dream. In my dream someone came and picked me up from my sleep and flew me all the way down, showing me the highway and even an unused railway bridge which only the locals know about.

When I went to work the next day and told my friend about my helpful visitor, she would not – and still does not – believe me. She couldn't believe that I had not been there before.

Tanya, Australia

Was this an angel or perhaps Tanya's spirit guide? Obviously they were concerned enough that they felt it was worth showing her the way. It really makes you think, doesn't it? Might Tanya and her friend have got lost on the way? Could this have been dangerous or simply inconvenient? Either way we'll never know, but the fact that they arrived at their journey's end safely … and nothing actually happened, is magical in itself! Out-of-body experiences can be most helpful, like this one, but often occur when we have a strong need to be somewhere or be with someone.

Have you had a spiritual helper appear to you with good news or helpful advice while you sleep? I often receive information in this way. My own angels and guides (and deceased loved ones) seem better able to reach out to me when I sleep.

Even though they communicate with subtle thoughts and feelings all day long, I much prefer the more 'concrete advice' which occurs during sleep. I literally see my angels when I dream: they come over for a chat or show me things to make sure I get the message. There is no confusion when my guides speak to me, although I'll admit not all spiritual helpers work in the same way … some have a more 'hands-off' approach, preferring for us to work things out for ourselves. An American friend tells me that her spirit guides like to give her puzzles to work out … now that would drive me nuts, I'm sure! Good job we aren't all alike.

A LITTLE HEALING COMFORT

We've looked at all sorts of different types of angel healing in this book, but not every experience need be dramatic. Sometimes the best sort of healing is when our loved ones bring a little comfort into our lives. The encounter can be subtle but when a deceased loved one draws close to your physical body you are able to 'feel' them as well as sense them. They don't need to speak and it doesn't matter if you can't see them.

Human beings are great at picking up information by sense. Have you ever walked into a creepy house or been in a situation where you felt on full-alert? Sometimes we just know when we are in danger just by picking up on the change of energy in the atmosphere.

You know when you and a loved one are thinking the same thing … listening in to each other's thoughts? You might even finish a sentence the same way, or laugh and say, 'I was just going to say the same thing.' When you have lived with a person for many years, that connection isn't broken on death. Thoughts and minds continue to connect as one. If you sense strongly that a deceased loved one is with you, then he or she probably is. Here's Vivienne's experience which she sent me in an e-mail.

Warm Knees

In the two years since my husband passed he has been protecting me. I was never comfortable being on my own at night, but even though he has passed I feel totally protected. Eleven weeks after his passing I was getting ready to see a psychic medium to have a reading and I was hoping that my husband would bring a message from the other side. The whole time I was getting ready the bathroom light flickered and only stopped when I acknowledged his presence. I was delighted.

Other strange things have happened, too, and I often wonder if he had a hand in them. There have been the pictures that needed straightening, and the dent in the bed that looks like someone has been sat there. In the spring there is often a strong scent of daffodils, inside the house!

His most obvious presence is at night when I ask him to warm my cold knees – a standing joke in our household as I was always warming *his* cold knees after he'd been working in his workshop late at night. At first it was just a warming sensation over the knees, even though my skin still felt cold. Now it is my whole legs and they feel like there is a weight on them, as though he is lying on top of me. It is a very comforting feeling knowing he's never far from me.

Once I even saw his face: he looked about 30 years old (although he was 56 when he died). I have just read your book *An Angel Saved My Life* and I am now reading *An Angel by My Side*. I think these are very creditable accounts of others' experiences of contact with their loved ones. I look forward to the day when I can contact my soulmate without having to use a medium.

Vivienne, New Zealand

It sounds like Vivienne's husband is already visiting without a medium, doesn't it? By the way, spirits nearly always appear to us as younger than when they died, it's like they're saying, 'Look how well I am now ...' For the record, spirits can appear to us pretty well any way they want, but most will use the appearance of their most recent earthly body ... that is, the way they looked when they died, but the best possible version of their Earth self.

Who are the angel helpers in these next stories?

'Keeping-an-eye-on-me' Angels!

When I was a teenager I was cohabiting with a violent man, and after an argument he beat me so badly that just after I left our flat I fell over in the front garden into the snow. As I lay there in the snow I tried to lift my head up and get up but I had no energy to do so. I remember lying face-down looking at the white ground and feeling very, very warm and sleepy. My last thought before I fell asleep was how happy and peaceful I felt and how I could just go to sleep, and that is exactly what I did.

Just before I woke up I was sitting in a very white room and someone came into this room and told me, 'You cannot stay here, you have to go home. It's your dinner time; you must go home and eat.' I cannot remember who told me this but I remember thinking, 'No, I'm not hungry, I want to stay here.' Suddenly there was a very, very bright light and I had this overwhelming feeling of being hungry. The light was shining so bright and I felt so hungry. I opened my eyes and the bright light was still there, and as my eyes began to focus things like ceiling lights, curtains and pretty flowers on the curtains started to come into focus. There was someone with me and they were telling me I was OK, I was in hospital ... unbeknownst to me I had been in a coma-like state for five days after being admitted to the hospital with severe hypothermia. I had been found face-down in the snow by a milkman making his deliveries and I had been in the snow for over 12 hours. The milkman thought I was dead. Just before I had woken from my coma I had spoken out loud, 'Is it dinner time?'

I never contacted or found out who the milkman was who found me in the snow that night, but it certainly wasn't my time to go.

Another strange thing happened when I was 16. I used to go for walks in the very early hours of the morning, mainly to escape from arguments at home with my violent boyfriend ... I had been walking around Norwich city centre and my boyfriend had found me and was in the process of getting me to go home ... for no reason I looked up at a house we were passing and on the porch stood an angel just standing looking down at me ... this was not the normal type of angel that people talk about in books, no glowing wings or shiny halo ... this angel was at least 10 feet tall and jet black from head to foot. At first I thought it was a statue on the porch; it was November time and maybe it was some form of early Christmas decoration? I stared at this angel for what seemed like minutes, but was most likely only a few seconds ... as we passed it I was telling my boyfriend, 'Look at that.' I turned to look back and nothing was on the porch.

I have passed the same house many times since my teenage years and have never seen it or any statue again, nor have I found any explanations for seeing this.

I have had many little experiences as an adult of seeing faces when I close my eyes to sleep, also I have very vivid dreams and I feel emotional around certain people or areas but I am also very fearful and become scared when things like this happen to me – but I do believe someone watches out for me and protects me. I always find when I'm most in need someone or something helps me and I never feel totally alone. I just wish I could overcome my fears to learn more from my experiences.

Naomi, England

IN SICKNESS ... AND IN HEALTH

It's amusing, really: if you remember your sister as she was when she died, with silvery hair and a walking stick, and she appears in your dream by skipping into view with full-length glossy black hair, she is showing you how she would have liked to have looked … her idea of her 'perfect' self. The spirit 'body' will appear glowing with health, whole and without a single sign of any illness that plagued her in life.

My own father appeared in a variety of ways after he passed (I have written up his story in my book *Call Me When You Get to Heaven*, co-written with my sister Madeline Richardson). Sometimes Dad looked as he did when he passed – complete with walking stick and spectacles, and smelling of mints! – especially when he appeared to his grandchildren, but mainly he looked younger. He jumped around and even skipped, seemingly to show us that now that he was dead, he was well and recovered!

KEEPING A PROMISE TO COMMUNICATE FROM HEAVEN

Joel and Albert had HIV. Some people will recall that in the early days of diagnosis, in many countries HIV was considered a death sentence. Medical advances have since shown that this need not always be the case, and many people with the diagnosis live long, full lives. However, anyone who lives with a serious illness may well have considered their own mortality, and Joel and Albert were no different. Joel says, 'We swore we would try to signal one another as an assurance of life after death. We both wanted to believe there was something beyond this world and its suffering.'

After Albert passed on he began sending signs and messages … many of them to Joel and others. Joel was even occasionally able to hear messages (in his head) from his close friend, and received other signs, too, including a translucent light that appeared over his bed, and hummingbirds which regularly appeared as Albert's special sign. (The full story is in the book *Signals* by Joel Rothschild.)

IN DANGER AND DISTRESS
This story took place many years ago ...

Angel Driver

My father passed away in 1972, aged 58. He had been ill on and off for many years. My father used to work in the steelworks in Scunthorpe and was also a part-time chimney sweep.

In 1975 my brother Tom and his family emigrated to Australia. They decided to go by sea from Southampton, so Mother and I travelled down with them (arranging to stay in Southampton overnight) and watched them board the ship. They were due to sail mid-afternoon, but this kept being put back. The day went on and still they hadn't sailed. Mother and I were determined to wave them off as they started their long journey. The boys went to bed because they were aged 11, 8 and 4. Mother and I stood our ground and in the end we were the only ones on the quayside. Around 2 a.m. the ship finally set sail. We waved like mad, screaming and shouting from the quayside, and my brother and sister-in-law were doing the same from the ship.

We carried on like this until they were out of sight. I always remember my father making me listen to a song on the radio by Charley Pride called 'Crystal Chandeliers', and as we watched the ship sail into the distance Mother and I looked at each other and both agreed the ship looked just like a crystal chandelier!

It was only then that we started to realize we were in a strange town in the middle of the night. We had to find our way back to our guest house for what was remaining of the night but we had no idea where to go. Obviously there was no one around at this time so we started to walk towards the town hoping we could catch a taxi. Out of nowhere appeared an old van with a man driving. He was dressed in a flat cap and had a white scarf around his neck. I never did see his face. The man asked us where we were going and if we would like a lift. As we were together we had no hesitation in accepting.

When we arrived at the guest house, we expressed our thanks. We quickly checked the house number and turned round to wave to the man but we couldn't see the van anywhere. It was a long straight road with no turn-off and very few vehicles parked along it. We couldn't believe it and then suddenly we said to each other, 'Can you smell soot?' My father used to have an old van for his chimney-sweeping rounds so that he could put the bags of soot into it when he had finished his work! Added to this he always wore a flat cap and a white neck scarf. I'm sure he was with us on the quayside to watch his son leave the UK for a new life and also to make sure that Mother and I made it safely to our destination. His visit made this very special family occasion so much more special. We know that father was our angel driver!

My mother passed away in 1991 and I have often sensed and smelled her near me. I now ask for help from the angels and quite often receive signs, including white feathers. It is the best medicine ever, so thank you so, so very much for writing your books and I will read more as you write them.

Betty, England

Thank *you*, Betty – I will keep writing books to inspire and uplift you ... and all my readers! OK, enough of that for now. It's time for another fascinating reader's experience.

Healing Helper

My father's mother (my grandmother), died in childbirth; she was Irish. She had seven children. I did not know her, and don't recall ever seeing a picture of her.

When my father was stationed at the Royal Naval Docks I once felt a woman standing beside me even though she wasn't visible ... all except the cuff of her sleeve. She became my 'friend'. I continued to feel her around throughout my life. Once when I had a near-death experience she came to me on the ward. All I could physically see again was the pretty cuff of a sleeve. One day my cousin gave me a photograph of two children elegantly dressed, one was sitting on a woman's knee, and one on a stool. The woman had the same jaw line as me and looked like my dad's younger sister. Then I spotted the cuffs, which I felt had been with me since birth and all my life. It was now too late to ask my father but I know that she is with me still ... but I do wonder if she is my grandmother or Dad's sister?

I have the photograph on my dresser at home now and she is the first person I see when I wake and the last person I see at night. If I am in danger she comes to bring me comfort ... and I can smell the scent of old roses on her hands. She will come for me when it is my time to pass and I believe she is always there for me.

Pauline, England

Seeing a cuff is one thing ... hearing a voice is quite another! Like many of the authors of stories in this book, Sarah works as a carer.

Bring Me a Sign

Well, where do I start? I'm a 30-year-old mother of two boys and have been married for 10 years. I have always worked as a health care assistant and dealt with death over and over again. In the past I've seen silhouettes of people as well as heard, seen and sensed things. I've always dismissed these experiences because I believe in God and I've felt that to pick up on psychic things was a bad thing. Now I realize it's not!

I lost my dear dad on New Year's Eve, 2006. He had a heart attack. My father had been sick for months but would do nothing about it: I still don't understand why. My world came crashing down when he died.

Over the years I've saved so many lives but I could not save my dad's. Every day for two weeks before the funeral I would cry out to Dad, 'Just let me know you are OK, then I will be OK; please show me a sign, let it snow, then I can be strong.' I even told the vicar what I said to Dad, but he didn't approve of my request.

Well, on the day of the funeral we were at my brother's house. Everyone was there; even his family from Germany had travelled over. Some I knew and some I didn't. I wanted to use the toilet before it was time to go, so I went upstairs and, strangely, the door was locked. I knocked and knocked but no one answered, so then I called out and tried the door but the door was locked so I waited.

A short while later an auntie came up the stairs to use the bathroom too and I explained someone was in there, and that they might need some time to themselves. We chatted for a while about my dad, then my sister-in-law came up to use the bathroom. I told her we were waiting but I was getting desperate now. I called out again and no one answered, so I just pulled the handle down and pushed the door when a voice said quite clearly, 'It's me.' I thought it was my brother's voice so we hurried downstairs (I felt embarrassed for him with us waiting outside the door like that). As I walked through the living room into the kitchen, my brother was sitting at the table. I started to panic and looked around to make sure everyone else was downstairs. Everyone was wondering what was wrong with me and then I was hysterical and crying to my brother about the voice. My auntie and sister-in-law had heard it, too!

My brother calmed me down and went upstairs to look. This time the door opened right away and no one was there. I'd been mistaken – it wasn't my brother but it was my dad. I was not afraid of my dad! It was the thought that he might not know he was dead. After I calmed down I started to laugh. This was the sort of clear sign I had been looking for, and there were witnesses, too. I thanked Dad and managed to get through the day as strong as ever.

After that I used to see the outline shape of Dad in the garden or in the house; sometimes I could smell him, too, and I always said hello. One night I was woken with a kiss on the side of my mouth. I thought it was my husband and then realized he was asleep. I closed my eyes then and I started to see my dad. He did not look the way he did when he died; he was smiling. The whole vision was in black and white and I found myself talking to him in my head and telling him that

I could see him. It was all over in a few minutes. I have never seen or heard from Dad since.

I now realize it's not wrong to see these things … and that I was not mad. I intend to carry on investigating the afterlife and am no longer afraid.

Sarah, England

Here's another great story – this one is about a special dream-visit from a friend whom Anneka cared for in a nursing home. Anneka clearly made quite an impact!

Crisps!

Eddie was a lovely man and trusted me a lot. He used to give me crisps every day. Every day at the start of my shift I'd stop and visit him. Then one day I was on my way out when Eddie shouted, 'Pack of crisps?' I told him I was on my way home and would get them later on. The next morning I awoke after having had the weirdest dream! A young man was sat beside me and he had the most amazing blue (and familiar) eyes. He told me I knew him and he was smiling at me. I knew he was a ghost but no one else could see him in the dream.

Then the location changed and I was saying goodbye to him. Just as he walked away he handed me a pack of my favourite crisps and said, 'I didn't want you to be without.' I couldn't get the dream out of head. My mum works at the same place as me and she rang with the news that Eddie was dead. I was so upset but then I caught on! It was Eddie in the dream but he'd appeared to me as a much younger and healthier-looking man.

A few days later I was asked by a senior member of staff
to clear out Eddie's room. I wondered why she'd chosen me
when there were hundreds of staff working there, but I felt it
had something to do with the fact that I was the only one Eddie
allowed in his room when he was alive. A week later I was
thinking about Eddie and before I went to bed I asked for a
sign that Eddie was OK. That night I had another weird dream.
I was in the care home not too far from Eddie's old room. Eddie
was there and he told me 'they don't let people out for very
long "up here".' We walked up to his old room and I told him
someone else had it now and he was OK about it. He'd just
come back to let me know he was OK and then he left again.
How weird was that?

Anneka, England

It was very weird, Anneka, but lovely, too!

Here is another helper from the other side – Cynthia's dad
was no doctor but in heaven he could clearly see something his
daughter couldn't!

Is That You, Dad?

I must tell you about an experience I had in 2002, but I will
go back a bit to let you understand how it came about.

In 1988 I lost my father to a very sudden death. He'd
had a heart attack. It affected me badly as we were not on
speaking terms at the time, due to his drink problem. Fast
forward to 2002 when, over a couple of days in October, I
started feeling quite unwell. I was breathless, I had a sore
chest and nausea and I was off work just lying about the
house. All at once I became aware of a very strong perfume

smell. It seemed to be following me, and I was asking other people in the house if they could smell it too because it was so strong, but no, I was the only one.

Later when I went to bed I fell asleep almost immediately, then just as suddenly I seemed to wake up. I'm not sure of all the details but there was someone standing at the bottom of my bed and I have to say it looked like my dad and sounded like him, too. In my dad's voice I clearly heard him say, 'I was only 52 ... you need to get this sorted.' Then he was gone.

The following morning I had a heart attack and ended up in the hospital. Doctors discovered that I needed coronary stents and the operation was scheduled for the start of 2003. For reasons unknown, I took unwell in the December and ended up getting admitted for surgery on 8th December instead ... the anniversary of my dad's passing. I had my operation on 14th December (which had been the day of my dad's funeral). I have been well since then but often ask myself if it really was my dad that night.

... By the way, I love angels and have them all over my house and even in my car!

Cynthia, Scotland

How do you feel about these real-life experiences? You know they are real, right? OK, let's have a look at some more!

My Daughter Is Protected by My Deceased Friend

An experience I had opened my life up to angels. My story is not a great miracle but is something I hold precious to me. I was in hospital having my fifth child. I did not know the gender of my child but believed I was having a boy and had

picked the name Daniel Craig after two close friends who
were killed in separate accidents a couple of years apart.
I was not in a relationship with the baby's father (he had
forgotten to tell me he was married!) and had contemplated
giving up the baby for adoption. My doctor had advised me
not to make that choice at the time and wait until I had the
baby to decide what I wanted to do. I was employed full-time
and my family and friends had been giving me advice, saying
there was no reason I could not raise the baby alone, etc.,
and that as I was working I could afford to keep the baby.
Anyway, I had a caesarean under anaesthetic and was waking
up in the recovery room when I had a strange experience.
I did not know I had given birth to a baby girl when I felt
someone standing near my bed. The person (who I believe
was my deceased friend Craig) told me I had a girl and to call
her Karlee (he even spelled the name out for me). I'd had my
last child (a girl) by caesarean and never had this experience.
Up until this stage I had not chosen any girls' names. I then
woke up and asked the nurse what I had had and she told
me a girl. I drifted back off and then asked another nurse
who told me the same thing. A few days later in my hospital
room I was thinking about my experience (I was under the
influence of morphine via drip for the first two days) and the
name I had chosen for my daughter and I realized I have
a sister called Karole and a sister called Lee-Anne, which
together make the name Karlee. I had never even considered
using the name before this experience or even thought about
putting their names together! I have another sister named
Melinda whom I had named one of my previous daughters
after. Karlee was born nearly four weeks early (I had problems

and was in hospital trying to stop early labour) and her date of birth is the same date as Craig's who tragically died. I today believe he chose the name for my daughter and she was born on his birthday so he is never forgotten to me. I never gave her up for adoption after that experience.

I recently went and visited the cross on the side of the road where he had the accident and put a flower on it (I always make sure I go at least once a year as close as possible to his birthday or the day he died). As it was five years (I have never forgotten him in that time) since he died I asked him to give me a sign that he knew I was there and would never be forgotten to me and could hear me when I talk to him (I am more open to this after my hospital experience and regularly talk to him like he is right beside me). Anyway, in a matter of seconds the truck Karlee's father used to drive drove past (I had not seen it for a long time) and as Karlee was born on Craig's birthday I believe that was a sign he knew and would always be there beside me. Thank you for the chance to tell you my story. I haven't told people before as others may not believe as I do. Karlee is now two and a half years old.

Grandpa Guardian

I have recently lost my father; however, my young granddaughter has been speaking to an older man when she is on her own in her bathroom, and has told my daughter that it is 'great-grampa'. She states that she hears him through her head and he is telling her to wear her seatbelt, which she hates doing. She also states that he is English even though we live in Wales. My dad's family were all originally from the city of Bath and he was very proud of the English connection.

152

Therefore could the location of the bathroom be a significant link or a sign due to the water and bath? I feel that at her young age she is not old enough to make this up.

Anastasia, Wales

Please Don't Leave Me?

Some 18 months ago I suffered a severe stroke. As I lay in the emergency ward being treated I remember someone saying to me, 'Please don't leave me.' I'm not sure if it was my husband or my guardian angel at the time, as after I heard these words I started to come back to life. When I was back on the ward I remember my husband saying to me, 'We nearly lost you.' I replied, 'No, not when my guardian angel told me I was not going anywhere just yet.' I thank my angel every day for her help and I truly believe that my faith in my angels saved me on this fateful day. Every day when the nurses spoke to me I told them, 'Believe in your angels and they will watch over you.' They all used to look at me as though I was on another planet even when I told them that my angel saved me as I should have died on that day back in March 2009.

Margaret, England

The Olive Branch

My father-in-law recently passed away, it was actually a week before Easter Sunday. He was a very kind, gentle man and never spoke a bad word about anything or anyone. It was the eve of Palm Sunday and my in-laws live four hours away from us. We were at my son's Holy Communion commitment mass at our parish church near our home. It was 6 o'clock and my youngest son had just been handed an olive branch to take into the mass. We told him it had special significance and to look after it. We got home from the mass at 7:30 p.m. and received a phone call from my husband's sister around 8:45 p.m. to say that Dad had taken a bad fall while picking olives and had sustained serious head injuries, and that they were on their way to hospital with him. Soon after finding this out, my husband left to drive the four hours to get to his parents' place, leaving around 9:15 p.m. It seemed so coincidental, when we had not been to a mass for Palm Sunday for many, many years, that the olive branch was given to us at the exact time that my father-in-law had apparently taken his fall while picking olives. Then at around 9:40 p.m. something said to me, 'Tell them that I love them,' and my first thought was 'Is that Dad?' I refused to believe it at first, thinking my mind was playing tricks on me, and commenced to say, 'No, you are going to be OK, you will get to tell them.' I brushed it aside, not wanting to believe it. I received a call from my husband around 1 in the morning to say that his dad had passed away. When I asked my sister-in-law the time that he had died, she said it was around 9:45 p.m. I then relayed the message to her and she started crying knowing that he must have passed the message on to me as he could not speak himself. I still knew that he had more that he wanted to say; however, a month or so went past until one day I felt the need to sit down and talk with him. I could feel his presence and he passed on a long message to me to give to the family. It is funny because I could not hear his voice, but all the words were just coming out and I was quickly writing them down on paper. I remember thinking 'I could not have just thought this up, it happened too quickly.' I felt it gave the family some

closure on his death and it brought a lot of peace. Another
month or so later I had a very vivid dream of him when he
was in his younger years. He looked so well, handsome
and happy and was up on a field on a green mountain, and
walking down the hill were three men, which when I thought
about it later must have been his father and two brothers who
had passed away. They were chatting amongst themselves
and Dad was smiling down at them, like he had just spoken
to them. He could not see me; I was just watching this all
happen. It felt so beautiful and was so peaceful to see. The
feeling has remained with me for a long time. Now I still feel
his presence occasionally and ask for his guidance or help
when I need it.

Angela, England

From a Nurse's Point of View ...

*Birth, life, and death ... each took place
on the hidden side of a leaf.*
– Toni Morrison

Doctors, nurses and health care workers are often in the unique position of being close to or sitting with folk when they pass over to the other side of life. These days we find the very thought of death a terrifying prospect, but for those who sit with the dying it's often a very magical and special experience, especially if we share in those final moments. The death from the earthly realms is but a birth into the heavenly realms. Like a butterfly that emerges from its cocoon, the death of one form leads to a beautiful new life.

Carers who are at the bedside during the transition may often witness paranormal phenomena: shafts of light, angel music, flowery scents and visions of angels and spirits.

The loss of a loved one is the most stressful experience, yet for the dying it can be the most wonderful of experiences. Once the spirit passes through and out of the physical body, we're told that pain no longer exists, and even as this process begins the dying person begins to share experiences that they have seen, heard and felt. Strangely I have many, many nurses, healers and carers attend my workshops. They tell me they want to better understand the spiritual aspects of dying so that they can help patients more. Isn't that wonderful?

What's it like to be with someone when they pass over? Let's talk to some experts.

Final Hours from a First-hand Witness

I have a very privileged position in the hospital, privileged because I occasionally find myself sitting with a patient as they pass from this life into the next. For many years I have been witness to the phenomena that occur when a person dies, and for this reason I sought to develop myself psychically to allow myself to fully understand this special spiritual experience.

As you may know a human being has an aura, a colourful energetic radiance that surrounds us all. This is also true of the dying person, although the aura is not quite as radiant and much harder to see. In my experience the aura dulls quite quickly as death approaches; colours merge into frequently indescribable hues, often not completely dissipating for up to one hour after a person dies.

During a night shift I received a call from one of my wards asking me to come and review an elderly female patient. The staff nurse was concerned that the patient was deteriorating. I entered the patient's bedroom to see a frail woman lying unconscious in her hospital bed. Her breathing was shallow and her skin pale, her aura was a faded smoky grey and seemed small against the crisp whiteness of her pillow case.

I called the staff nurse and asked her to contact the relatives, expressing that the woman was near to death. I sat by the bed gently stroking the patient's hand while softly reassuring her that her relatives would soon be there. While sitting quietly I noticed a light at the corner of my eye. The room was dimly lit but the light was bright blue and seemed localized to the corner of the room just to the left of the window. As I softened my vision I could make out shapes at the centre of the light, shapes which manifested as human in stature and volume, although strangely lacking in physical/ facial characteristics, practically shadow-like in appearance. The light moved stealthily towards the foot of the bed and lingered, silently and without movement. I glanced at my patient: her face was now mellow, with the hint of a smile. As she took her last, gasping breath her aura seemed to pale against the pillow. Turning to face the light I noticed it had also dimmed and was drawing back from the foot of the bed, the figures no longer discernible in the failing light.

The room felt peaceful and I considered myself truly honoured to have experienced such a beautiful phenomenon, assured by the belief that our loved ones greet us at the end of this life and deliver us safely and securely into the next.

Terri, England

Terri's patient didn't speak or seem to share her experience in any way, but many do. Kerry is a nurse I have known for many years. Naturally she doesn't share patients' personal details for confidentiality reasons. Here is her story:

Angel Collects a Dying Man

A patient I was looking after called me into his hospital room. We all knew he was in his final hours, and unfortunately medicine could no longer cure or prolong his life.

He wanted to share his experience with me and told me he'd seen an angel in his hospital room, and explained that he was nearly ready to go. He was convinced of what he'd seen and said, 'You may not believe me but I really did see her.'

I told him I *did* believe him and that I do believe in angels. The patient told me he wasn't scared of dying and it (heaven) seemed a nice place to go to.

The gentleman wanted to sort out a couple of things before he left, and as I went off shift he asked someone to write a letter for him. Right afterwards he passed on. My colleagues told me that he went peacefully.

Kerry, England

In the final days of life, a family friend told me that she had seen her room filled with singing angels. She crossly told me they had awoken her during the night, which I found rather amusing. I assumed she'd be more entranced by the angelic sight than put out by the fact that they'd woken her!

Here's another story about a young woman who had the role of sitting with the dying. Over time you learn a lot about what happens before and sometimes immediately after we pass to spirit.

Reunited

When I was 19 years old I was working in a nursing home for the elderly and mentally ill. I loved my job but up until then I had never witnessed a death. Part of my job was to sit with the residents when their time was coming. The one woman who has stayed in my memory was a woman I will call Peggy. Now, Peggy was a lovely woman if you got her on a good day, but she was slightly absent-minded sometimes, which I guess does come with age. When it was my turn to sit with Peggy she was sleeping most of the time but then all of a sudden she woke up and looked straight ahead of her. She was clearly seeing someone that I couldn't see. Then Peggy spoke, saying to the figure in front of her, 'Mam, you're back!'

I knew there was no mistaking the fact that she was looking at her mum in spirit. Then Peggy went on to hold a conversation with her mother; some of it I wasn't able to make out, but the gist of it was that her mum and other family members had come to take Peggy to the afterlife.

The look on Peggy's face was one of pure love for her family, and peace. Peggy never said another word to staff from that moment on, she would only speak when family visited her in spirit, but there was no mistaking they were there for her.

When the time came for Peggy to join them she held out her hand and said thank you to her mum for showing her the way, and for coming back. Peggy went unconscious for a few hours before she finally passed on.

Since that time I have sat with and nursed many elderly patients when they've passed over, and from what I've seen it is very clear that there is an afterlife. Loved ones do visit us. On a few occasions I've known about their passing when I've been off duty, even if it was unexpected. One day I started to get visits from a particular woman in my dreams and I knew she was trying to tell me something. At the time I'd been off sick but I found out a week or so later that this woman had passed away at the time she appeared in my dreams.

Elaine, England

Sitting at the bedside of the dying is a very special job; it's also exhausting emotionally, especially if the person is known to you. A friend has recently lost her mother and she was holding her as she took her final breath. All she has seen since, every time she closes her eyes, is that final breath and she goes over and over it in her mind ... readers who have been through this experience will understand ... yet as I have explained before, sometimes our relatives will wait until we leave the room before they leave their earthly bodies for good! It's like they wait for those final moments of privacy.

Don't feel bad if you're not around at the time a loved one crosses over. It's impossible for us to be at the bedside of every relative who dies. It's just not logical to think we can. As we've seen from the experiences in this chapter – our loved ones are never alone when they die. There is always someone with them, even if that person is invisible to those of us on this side of life!

WHO'S WAITING ON THE OTHER SIDE?

Sometimes the dying see just one person (at first) but later they will encounter a whole host of people, either immediately they pass or even literally waiting around the bedside. When it's 'our time', we are told so. A guide or loved one will beckon, and literally say, 'It's your time ... [fill in the name of your deceased loved one here] ...' Sometimes the dying person has a choice to stay or go which indicates that not every 'death' date is set in stone.

My uncle came to me in a dream and warned me that my dad had between 3 and 18 months to live. Dad died 3 months later and none of us blamed him one bit that he 'left' when he did. His elderly body was ravaged by ill-health. Why stay longer?

Later Dad appeared to several of us (his daughters) in dreams to explain why he left the Earth-plane. Perhaps he felt guilty for leaving 'early' ... but he needn't have. He showed us how he would have been in pain had he lived, but most of all he demonstrated how fit and well he was now he was in his spirit body. Dad's visitations included lots of jumping, hopping and skipping! We all understood how tired he was in his earthly body. It was 'his time' ... and those of us who are left behind must remember that our loved ones are greeted by just as many who love them on the other side.

The welcome home (to heaven) party might include the following who've gone before us:

- **husband, wife, boyfriend, girlfriend and lovers**
- **parents**
- **uncles and aunts**
- **brothers and sisters**
- **cousins**
- **friends (even some you haven't thought of in years)**
- **old school friends**
- **old work colleagues**
- **teachers**
- **your guardian angel**
- **your spirit guides**
- **pets**
- **beings from other realms or planets that have been working with you**
- **members of your soul group (spirits you incarnate with over many lifetimes).**

PEOPLE WE DON'T WANT TO MEET 'THROUGH THE LIGHT'

Your 'welcome committee' will include people who have touched your life, people you love and want to greet you. People who have hurt you in life (physically or mentally) will *not* be amongst this group. Don't be concerned if you've had several intimate partners – there won't be a fight at the pearly gates! Exclusive sexual partners that we have in life translate to a completely different relationship heaven-side where spiritual relationships now take over. It's likely that these numerous partners are people we have lived with (in different combinations) over many lifetimes anyway.

Later it might be possible to meet up with those we have harmed or who harmed us (if we want) for apologies or explanations as to why they, or we, behaved towards each other as we did in this life. It's only once we pass to the light that we see the full picture of what we did, said and how we lived our lives. We also find out how we have hurt others during that lifetime. If you were abused in life, for example, your abuser will not be permitted to approach you at this time. It's surprising how many people worry about this. You are safe and protected by your guides and angels.

As we've seen, this committee might start gathering in the hours, days and weeks before you pass over. When the dying slip in and out of consciousness they often witness their heavenly visitors. It's such a comfort to know this is happening. They'll be well taken care of in heaven, too.

Now we know that our angels and deceased loved ones are waiting heaven-side, let's discover how they help us in secret and clever ways from their vantage-point ...

Angel Voices

Thy voice is a celestial melody.
– Henry Wadsworth Longfellow

Has an angel spoken to you? Have you heard that sweet voice speak to you in warning? What are angel voices: a typical angelic choir sound, or an actual voice speaking to you either in your head or literally in your ear? Many people have one-off types of experiences when they are at their lowest ebb – an experience that happens one time and never again. The voice appears from nowhere to warn or protect you ... sometimes the voice is reassuring or nurturing, simply letting you know that everything is going to be OK.

Your angelic voice might be familiar to you – reminding you of your recently deceased aunt or an old friend who passed away many years ago. Maybe your angel is the spirit of a loved one come back to help when times are challenging. To some people the 'voice' comes as more of a strong internal thought or feeling, yet still we understand the message, and the feeling that comes with it ... often so urgent we feel bound to follow the message it brings.

Job 'Agency' Angel!

Many years ago my husband was in danger of losing his job. It was very close to Christmas and we had three young children so I was terrified. My husband was in serious denial and just kept saying, 'It will be OK, they won't finish me … they need me.' As the date got closer he suddenly realized it was actually a reality: he really was going to lose his job and we were frightened about what might happen next and how we were going to pay the bills.

Then one day a week before he was due to finish he was driving to work as usual and at the same time contemplating the reality of things to come. At the end of his shift that day he got in the car to drive home and, as he did so, he felt a hand on his shoulder and a voice telling him, 'It's going be OK' … but there was no one in the car!

Near the end of his journey, just five minutes from home, the voice returned. This time it told him to turn right, which he did, and to his amazement there was a bus depot down the little road which he didn't know about. Realizing there must be a reason for the message, he went in and told them he needed a job, and that he had experience. He could not believe they were actually looking for a vehicle body worker, which was his trade, and they offered him a job there and then, immediately, without him even having to apply or go for an interview.

My shocked husband couldn't wait to get home and tell me about his bewildering day! Mind you, he's still not sure he believes in angels – aren't men funny sometimes?

Collette, England

This next voice appeared just in time to help this woman at the altar. What happens when you have a panic attack in church?

Miracle Wedding, Miracle Baby

I was a single 33-year-old and had been told at 20 I would never be able to have children, as I have a tumour on my pituitary gland and this in turn stops me ovulating. After a few years of depression about this I got on with my life. I wasn't looking for a husband as I was barren, but I met and fell in love with my husband, whose name is Walter. It was love at first sight and I just knew that I would be with him forever, but I did not want this. Because of my feelings we fought all through our courtship, but Walter always said we would be married and I would have a child. This only made me more upset because all the gynaecologists and endocrinologists had been monitoring me for over 10 years and they all said no.

To cut a long story short, we twice set the date for our marriage but I cancelled it twice because, although I loved him dearly, he was everything I did not want in a man. He was egotistical, materialistic, European, aggressive and had black hair (I had never been out with anyone with black hair).

On the third date set for the wedding, everything was going fine and I was looking forward to our day. The night before the wedding we had the worst fight ever. My mum was staying with us that night and I tried to explain to her I was making the wrong decision and that I was going to call it off again. She just said it was nerves and to go ahead with it.

My father arrived in the morning and I was sure he would help me but no, he said I just needed a drink. The beauticians had arrived and I was crying so much all my make-up kept coming off. When the car arrived to take me to the church I had no make-up on but at least I was wearing the dress. I had decided that when I got to the church I would ask the priest to tell everyone to go home. No one would help me, including my girlfriends. They wouldn't believe that I didn't want to get married.

Now comes the strange part. When I arrived, everyone was seated. The priest waved me to walk down the aisle but at the same time I waved him to come to me. This went on between us for about a minute and then everything went very quiet like just before a storm. This very soft yellow-golden light appeared and engulfed the whole church, and a very calm deep voice told me not to worry: if I really did not want to marry Walter he would arrange for the priest to come up to me. The voice told me that he just wanted me to know that he knew how I was feeling, but confided that Walter loved me so much.

The voice offered to show me a miracle to prove what he was saying, suggesting I look at Walter's face, and that he would make him turn around. As I looked up Walter turned to me and his face was that of Walter at eight years old, exactly as I had seen in his photograph album.

The voice asked me to stop crying because I was luckier than most: I'd seen Walter at his very worst and that from this day on he would only get to be a better person. I realized that I was ready to marry at that moment. As I ran down the aisle I was under the impression everyone else had heard the voice as well, but no one had. I did marry him (without any make-up on) and we are very happy and I did go on to have a beautiful miracle baby girl, now 17 years old.

So who was this voice? Was it God? An angel? I do not know but I do believe in a higher being and for that I am so grateful.

Tanya, Australia

This is another experience of Jeanie's, whom we heard from earlier when she shared her experience about what happened when she came off her motorbike. After she lost her father he came back to reassure her that he was still around.

Don't Worry … Be Happy

My 'gift' has always been with me from a very early age; even my mother has the gift of premonition. One cold January day I had a feeling of doom, especially around my dad.

As the night was drawing in and the temperature started to drop even further the next-door neighbour Margaret came knocking on the door, very upset. She had been walking her dog in the woods near our home and something had spooked the dog, so the dog had run away and she couldn't find him. My father, being the man he was, said, 'You wait here and I will have a run out in the car to see if I can find him.' Two or three hours later there was still no sign of my dad. I just had this urge that I had to find him. I kept getting a vision of him sat in the car, very, very cold.

Margaret and I decided to go and search for Dad and the dog (Mum couldn't go anywhere as my brother was very young and he was in bed). We found Dad's car and Dad was inside; he was really cold and his face and lips were blue. I immediately grabbed the car blanket and kept telling Dad that I was there. Then it happened: I saw my father's spirit leave his body, but there was a light around him and I just knew he had died in my arms. When the ambulance crew arrived the police made me go home with them; Dad had died of a massive heart attack. It was completely shocking. Later that night as I lay in bed, my father came to me in a vision and told me not to worry and to be strong. I knew it was him because I could feel his presence.

Jeanie, England

Spirits are very impressive with their ability to bring signs to show us that they are still part of our lives. In my previous books I have listed all sorts of clues that they use to show us that they continue to exist: everything from bubbles and candle-wax shapes to messages in number plates and posters. Bird signs are one of my favourites, especially from robins, who seem to appear over and over again. There are a few robin stories sprinkled throughout my books. What do you think of this one?

Brave Little Feathered Friend

My mum, well, my foster mum, died in May this year. She was battling cancer but died very suddenly and unexpectedly at the time. It was a real blow to the whole family. I am still grieving, as we all are, but I have struggled to grieve because I have this barrier (of my own making) where I feel I don't have as much right to be sad as the rest of the family, her own children in particular.

I've pushed my grief to the back of my mind and thrown myself into work. Anyway, I was on holiday in France during the last two weeks of August and had read a couple of your books. I found them fascinating. I read that if you ask for a sign from the angels they will give you one. I asked for a sign and I asked, if my mum was out there, to let me know she was OK. The very next day when we were getting ready to go out for a meal a robin landed on the decking of the caravan. It was looking straight at me for what seemed like ages. It then came onto the table and stayed there for a while, then spent a bit more time on the terrace before flying away.

I told my family about it and that I thought it was the sign I had asked for, but they were very dismissive, so I suggested asking the robin to come back as proof. The next day as we arrived back from the beach the robin was sitting on our decking almost waiting for us. I took this as validation. It stayed for a while, then flew away. It might be coincidence but I have taken this as a sign. I wouldn't expect to see a robin in the middle of summer in France. It only appeared the two times I asked for a sign. It gave me a little comfort to know that maybe Mum is OK and still around me.

Nicky, England

Symbols from birds are just so reassuring and non-threatening (unless you are frightened of birds, that is!). Birds don't normally get so close, but in some of the visitation stories which people have shared wild birds have even jumped onto people's hands and appeared inside their houses. Sometimes normal garden birds appear at the 'wrong' time of year, which just adds to the mystery. Talking of mysteries, here is another story from a Facebook friend.

Coincidence?

Just thought you might like to hear my little story. I received a Facebook notification that a woman called Lisa Mitchell accepted my friend request today ... only I never sent a friend request to a Lisa Mitchell. The amazing thing is that my partner's grand-daughter died on 13th January 2010, aged three months. Her name was Lisa Mitchell.

Trisha

SAYING GOODBYE

When you are close to someone it's often possible to pick up a signal from their spirit that they have passed on. This might come in the form of a feeling, a visual clue or even the deceased themselves coming to let you know they have passed on.

Years ago my deceased uncle communicated to me that his god-daughter had died and was with him in heaven ... at the time the poor woman was in a coma after an accident, so she was physically still alive. Her family held out great hopes that she would recover, but several years later her physical body followed and she passed on, having never regained consciousness. The body needs the spirit to live and, as Uncle pointed out, the spirit was already on the other side with him.

This next story is very sad indeed. When this young boy passed over his mother knew right away that he had left her even though his physical body appeared to be still alive. I have included her whole story because you can see by the last conversation she had that the clues to his passing were all there ... did his spirit know he was leaving Earth?

Goodbye, Mum

When I was first married I was a silly girl because I was very naive about people. I was a country girl who found herself married at 18 and living in a town. I loved the country and always wanted to live there.

I married a guy who drove trains for a living and my parents hated him. Looking back, as I got older I understood why that marriage was doomed. I am a strong person and so was my dad. He controlled my life growing up and God help me if I didn't do as I was told. I later understood I was trying to get away from that control and used the first 'escape route' that came along ... and married him!

The man I married was someone I should have just left behind; I wish I had listened to my parents, but we are all wise in hindsight. Eighteen months after we married, I had my first child, a little boy we named Andrew. Then 17 months later his little brother Brian came along. I was so happy with my children because all I ever wanted was to be a good wife and mother.

However I still wasn't happy in my marriage. My husband was an abuser and a cheater, but as my parents had 'cut me off' for marrying him, it made it difficult to get away. I saw no escape.

After five and a half years I left and took my children with me. I didn't want my children to grow up in that environment thinking it was normal behaviour. I was offered the spare room in my boss' house so both my kids, aged four and two at the time, and I all crammed into a single bedroom with our meagre bits of furniture. My boss was not there a lot of the time and I minded his two kids when he was on shift-work, and kept the house clean, did the cooking and the gardening. It was an arrangement that worked for us both.

Many times I would be in the house doing housework or cooking and my boys would be playing in the yard with the 6-foot-high gate locked, yet their father would stop his car at the end of the driveway and the kids would scramble over the gate, run to him and get into his car; then he would drive away. I never knew where he would take the kids so would have to call my boss at work to bring his car home so I could go out and look for them. Most of the time he would come out in the car with me and help me look. It was a challenging situation!

After six months of this stress and nonsense (and a lot of other stupid things my ex did as well), my boss came home from work one day and told me we were moving house. I breathed a sigh of relief thinking that we would be moving elsewhere in the town so it would be harder for my ex to come and steal away the children. Then he told me he had given up his job and we were moving 400 kilometres away. I was stunned, and suggested that I take my kids and leave so he could keep his house and job, but he argued that he had become very close to all three of us and we all got along really well, and would like us to be a family.

After two years together we had our own little boy so now we had five children ... all boys. After the birth of my fifth child I suffered from postnatal depression for 18 months. It really put a strain on our relationship, but not as much as the strain of having to feed five children and having no money. One day I'd had enough and took the children to my mother's house (my father had already died by then and my mother had relented once I split from my first husband). I was glad of a couple of weeks' break to de-stress. While we were there my mother and my partner engineered a way to get the two of us back together. It worked. My partner got his old job back at the mill and we moved back to the mill-town ... later we built a house. My ex had been through two marriages by now and was now a little more amicable so I let him see the boys as often as he wanted.

Soon, Andrew was old enough to start intermediate school (he was 11) and as the school was about 4 kilometres from my house, and only 300 metres from his dad's, we agreed that he would have Andrew during the week. This worked out OK but I did miss my little boy so much. It was so hard not seeing him every day as I had been used to.

One weekend Andrew had come home and was playing with the other kids as usual. It was a normal day in every respect, but on the Sunday afternoon when his father came to collect him, he stood in the lounge doorway, looked at me from the other end of the hallway and said, 'Goodbye, Mum. I love you.' I thought it was a little odd at the time as he always said, 'See ya, Mum. I love you.' I replied, 'Don't you mean ... See ya?' and he said, 'No, I mean goodbye.' He gave me a big hug, hopped into his dad's car, and left.

Andrew was always a very spiritual boy but the other kids never understood that. He insisted on being allowed to go to Sunday school, and learn all he could about Jesus. All he ever asked for was his own white Bible, and to be baptized, although we never seemed to get round to either.

Two evenings later I got a call from the police asking if I had a son named Andrew. I was immediately alarmed, then he told me, 'Your son has been involved in a serious accident. He has been run over by a van and is in hospital, but I can't tell you any details.'

I was in shock. My partner rang the neighbour across the road to ask her to mind the other kids, then we raced to the hospital about 40 minutes away. Some months prior there had been a massive earthquake in our area and it had smashed the centre section of the bridge over the Whakatane River, so the Ministry of Works had installed a temporary 'Bailey Bridge' over the missing section, with traffic lights at each end. When we got to the bridge there were police cars with lights flashing and a long line of traffic. I assumed there had been another accident and expected that we would have to wait for hours to get through. Then a policeman came to our car and asked who I was. When he heard my name, he immediately radioed and started waving hand signals ... We had no idea what was going on. The officer came back and said that they'd been radioed a description of our car and my name, and told to hold all traffic until we got through!

Suddenly I was aware that my son's life was hanging in the balance and the whole situation became very frightening. We were allowed past the entire line of traffic, which was about 500 metres long.

When we got to the hospital we were escorted up to Intensive Care before being ushered into a small side-room. Soon Andrew's father and his wife arrived and joined us. We had arrived at 7 p.m. and the doctors came in to give us the update on what was going on ... we were not allowed to see Andrew at that time. We were told that his injuries were so severe and they were having difficulty trying to stabilize him. He had head injuries and the van had run over his torso so he also had internal injuries, but at that point the doctors didn't know to what extent. It was a very upsetting and tense time when all we wanted was to see our little boy. The staff were wonderful and kept giving us cups of tea. We just kept asking when we could see Andrew.

After two hours' wait, the doctors came and told us we could see him in half an hour, so we were geared for that, but that came and went and at 10 p.m. we asked why they were not allowing us in. They told us that they still had not stabilized my son, but said that as soon as they had, we could see him. The wait was agonizing.

Finally about 10 minutes later, as we sat there, I suddenly felt this amazing calm and warmth come over me and I knew Andrew was no longer our little boy: his spirit had gone from his body. I just sat and stared at the wall and the other three in the room thought I had gone barmy. At 10:30 p.m. they let us in to see Andrew, and although the machines were all that were keeping his body alive, his little body looked almost normal. He had lots of wires and tubes, as expected, but his head was heavily bandaged and one side of his face was a terrible mess. He also had the tyre marks across his torso where the wheel had run him over. We sat with him all night but I knew he just 'wasn't there'. In the morning the chief doctor came in and gave us the news that Andrew's main brain stem had been severed, his head trauma was so severe, and that he had substantial internal injuries and there was no way he would survive. But I was ready for this news; I already knew he had gone the night before.

Staggeringly the doctor then asked if we would consider donating his kidneys. We'd literally just been told he would die, but I immediately agreed to their request. His father was a little taken aback by my response and asked me why. Andrew and I had watched a documentary about transplants just a few weeks earlier. When a little Australian boy was dying and needed a bone marrow transplant, the only available donor was his baby sister. Andrew asked me at the time, 'Mum, what things do you transplant?' So we discussed the whole thing. He told me, 'I hope that if I ever needed a transplant, someone would be so kind to give me a kidney, even though I know their child would have died.' It was a very moving conversation and documentary, and it really affected Andrew, so I just knew it was the right thing to do.

Although my son was not the receiver of the donation I knew it was what he would have wanted. I'm so grateful for the skilled doctors who were able to use what my little son no longer needed, and give two other children a better life.

The day after Andrew died it was his brother Brian's tenth birthday. We'd had a death, a birthday and a funeral all within five days. My final gift to my son was to have him baptized in the hospital. I regretted not having done this for him while he was alive, but I know in my heart that he was where he was meant to be, and that a Bible was no use to him now and he had already somehow known. Maybe that was why Andrew came to this Earth? I don't know, but strangely my relationship broke down and I ended up with two little boys again.

Susanne, Australia

So sad ... I'm not sure that Susanne would have been comforted much to know in advance that somehow Andrew's spirit already knew it was his time. The loss of a child is the most shocking thing that can happen, but knowing that his loss saved the lives of two other children is a wonderful legacy.

Susanne also felt it when her brother passed over to the spirit-side. As with Andrew she picked up on his soul leaving his body.

Here is the story in her own words:

Sensing Spirit

Another more recent event in my life occurred in January 2009, but I need to back-track a little for you to get the story in perspective.

I have three brothers and two of them contracted the same form of cancer, non-Hodgkin's lymphoma, at around the same time. My middle brother Fred, 55, has always been a health food nut, so when he was diagnosed he immediately decided to treat his cancer the natural way through diet. My little brother Laurie, 51, decided to go with chemotherapy.

They both treated their cancers the way they wanted, but Laurie just got worse and worse, while Fred continued to improve. They both live in New Zealand, whilst I live in Australia. We are not a close family so don't see each other very much, nor do we keep in contact much either.

I live in a motel with 24 other residents and we have a social area we all call Melrose. Whenever there is something to celebrate, someone's birthday or a national event, we all get together and have a little celebratory party. On Australia Day in 2009, we were all outside celebrating during the evening, when a few minutes after 9 p.m. a strange calm feeling came over me and I immediately stopped talking. The person I'd been speaking to asked me why and I told her, 'Something is wrong ...'

For the next 10 minutes I was very disturbed and couldn't shake that feeling, so made my apologies and went back to my unit. I logged online and my fiancé (who lives in Indonesia) was online so we chatted and I told him something was wrong but I didn't know what it was. He is a very perceptive man and just said ... 'Just wait, you will know soon.'

About 5 minutes later I saw a message come across my screen from my little brother Laurie, which would have been around about 12:25 a.m. in New Zealand but was 9:25 p.m. in Australia. I thought, 'How very odd, why is such a sick man online at this hour of the night?' He never came online late. I opened the message and it was from his girlfriend. She told me that a few minutes past midnight, New Zealand time, my little brother Laurie had died. That was the exact time I felt his passing over.

He is at peace now with no more torturous pain suffered from the chemotherapy (my other brother, Fred, has been cancer-free for three years now).

Brothers and sisters, parents and children, lovers ... the connection is always strong and the spirit seems more aware than we ever know. Another really sad story, but the connection between the siblings was clearly closer than Susanne thought!

I thought you might like to read about her happy ending story, too! She told me:

Happily Ever After

I have a very good friend in New Zealand, Jo, who is a medium. She used to live next door when I lived in New Zealand. She once told me that my ex and I would not be together any more. (We split up two months later.) She also told me something I didn't take seriously at the time. She said, 'You will be alone for six to seven years, and then when you have learned the lessons you are meant to learn, a man will come into your life but it won't be what you expect. He will be from another culture and he will treat you with the kindness and love you deserve. He will be like nothing you have ever imagined and you will be together and happy for all your life.'

I actually laughed because I didn't believe her. I told her I'd had three marriages hit the wall and men were not on my shopping list, I was not interested. But you know, Jacky, she was absolutely correct. I was alone, although I did meet a few men along the way, none of whom made any impression on me at all. Then on Boxing Day in 2008 I received a message from an Indonesian man online with the most beautiful smile I had ever seen. I just couldn't stop looking at his smile, it just drew me in. We started to chat online and I thought, 'Gee, I'm lucky to have such a nice new friend.' We seem to be on the same page in so many ways.

We chatted and sent messages back and forth and I just looked at him as a new friend. I thought, in a month he will drop off and go on his way with his life, because reality said we live in different countries and we are both poor so will never get to meet anyway. However, he continued to contact me and I felt my attitude changing and becoming much more interested in him as a person. We had some fascinating conversations and we learned lots about each other's cultures. Then in February we were chatting more than ever and I was offered a temporary job looking after a family from Libya who were only in the country for two months. I worked hard on that job, long hours seven days a week. At the end of their stay they wanted to spend their last ten days in New Zealand so we all flew there.

After their holiday was over they flew back to Libya and I stayed on in New Zealand for two more days to see my family; then I flew back to Australia. When I logged on to my computer there were some really beautiful messages from my friend telling me how much he had missed me while I had been away. I'd made enough money working in my last job to fly to Bali for a holiday, and I needed it, too.

My friend arranged his annual leave so he could go to Bali as well. When I walked out of Denpasar International Airport, he was waiting for me in the hot sun. He'd been waiting for two hours. As soon as I saw him I felt an instant connection with him and just suddenly saw a future together with him. Yet up until that point I'd not even thought that way about him. To me it was magic ... Angel Magic. We spent a week touring around Bali on a motorcycle and it was the best holiday of my entire life. At the end of the week he proposed and I accepted. We had known each other for six months.

He is the most beautiful man in heart and soul I have ever met; he treats me with care, kindness, attention and the utmost respect, none of which I received from any man ever. I have since been to his home city, Jakarta, several times and met his family and special friends. I so want to go back there but at the moment I am working with immigration to get him here so that we can live together. I believe the universe had this planned, and I never doubt the universe.

I had forgotten about Jo's words until one day when I was at home and looking for something in a book, I found her reading: I had written her words down in a notebook years before, and you know ... she was spot on.

I believe in angels and feel the angels have helped and guided me for many years.

Susanne, Australia

I can't believe we're at the end of the book! With so many stories still to share with you ... Before we part again I wanted to share this special little experience. This woman was just a child when she saw her angel, but she's never forgotten it – and I know I wouldn't have, either.

Sucking Sweets!

When I was about six years old I was playing in our backyard with a friend. We were sucking sweets and, as I went to speak to her, the sweet slipped down my throat. It was terrifying and, worse, as I began to choke, my friend, who was only four, ran away leaving me on my own.

I remember starting to panic because I couldn't breathe, and then thinking 'I can't stand this any more.' No sooner had I wished it to stop than I found myself 'standing', perfectly calm, and wondering what had happened.

As I began to look around my attention was taken by a strange green circle that appeared on our old garden fence. It seemed to be revolving and as I watched this spinning light I was completely fascinated; it grew larger and larger until I could see a large green field. Then over the crest at the far end, children began to appear, walking slowly towards me.

In the centre of the group was a male figure dressed in a white robe, but I was more interested in the very pretty young girl who came skipping towards me with the loveliest smile. As she came closer she held out her hand to me, but I was shy and held back. I needed to inspect the other children to see if they all looked as friendly. I decided they did and put out my hand to take hers, but at that moment the man in white said something to the girl. She didn't look round but inclined her head towards him, smiled at me again and pointed to somewhere on my right.

As I turned I saw my mother coming out of our back door and she was running. I was conscious of a terrible feeling of disappointment as the young girl left, and as I looked back towards the spinning light, the field had already started to shrink. The children were waving goodbye and I remember crying out for them. It was too late and at the same time that they vanished, I found myself in my mother's arms. My friend had not run away but she'd gone to fetch my mum, who later told me I was lying on the ground when she got to me and I was blue in the face.

Barbara, England

Barbara had a near-death experience and she saw her guardian angel that day. The crowd of children were coming to meet her from the other side of life. Isn't it funny that she felt disappointed that she lived rather than died?! It just goes to show that death itself is less scary than life.

Life on our beautiful planet can be very short. Make sure you take care of yourself as best you can. Some of the accidents in this book are clearly avoidable (although not sucking sweets!) so make sure you keep safe and well. I'll ask your guardian angels to keep a close eye on you, too.

Wherever you are in life and whatever you're doing, know that you have your very own guardian angel watching over you. Never feel sad at being alone ... because you never are. Your angel loves you unconditionally and is always by your side. Don't forget to ask your guardian angel for a sign that he or she is close by ... perhaps your angel will leave you the gift of a fluffy white feather, just like some of the people in the book. Good luck, friends.

Also by this Author

Books

An Angel Held My Hand (Harper Element)

Angel Kids (Hay House)

An Angel by My Side (Harper Element)

An Angel Saved My Life (Harper Element)

An Angel Treasury (Harper Element)

Angels Watching Over Me (Hay House)

Dear Angel Lady (Hay House)

Angel Secrets (Octopus)

I Can See Angels (Hay House)

A Faerie Treasury (with Alicen Geddes-Ward; Hay House)

A Little Angel Love (Harper Element)

Call Me When You Get to Heaven (with Madeleine Richardson; Piatkus)

DVD

Angels (New World Music)

CDs

Meet Your Guardian Angel (guided meditations; Paradise Music)

Healing with Your Guardian Angel (guided meditations; Paradise Music)

Angel Workshop (workshop with meditations; Paradise Music)

Ghost Hunting Workshop with Barrie John (Paradise Music)

Crystal Angels (instrumental by Llewellyn,
cover notes by Jacky; Paradise Music)

Cards

Angels Secrets Cards (Octopus)

ABOUT THE AUTHOR

Jacky Newcomb, 'The Angel Lady', is a multi-award winning, *Sunday Times* bestselling author and columnist, and the UK's leading authority on Spontaneous Afterlife Communication.

Jacky is the expert the experts turn to, regularly interviewed in the national press and on radio and television. She has appeared on programmes such as *This Morning* and *LK Today* (The Lorraine Kelly Show).

Jacky was once editor of two paranormal and spiritual magazines, and is now the regular angel columnist for *Fate & Fortune* magazines, as well as writing for many others. She also specializes in interviewing celebrities about their own psychic and mystical experiences.

Jacky gives talks and runs workshops all over the country and has worked with many well-known names.

Jacky is a regular guest on local and national radio and is frequently interviewed in the national press including the *Daily Mail*, the *Daily Mirror* and the *Daily Express.*

Healed by an Angel is Jacky's twelfth book.

You can find Jacky on Twitter and Facebook, or write to her at:
Jacky Newcomb, The Angel Lady
c/o Hay House Publishers
292 Kensal Road
London W10 5BE

www.angellady.co.uk